Physical Education for

Physical Education for the Mentally Retarded

the Mentally Retarded

JOHN N. DROWATZKY, Ed.D.

Professor and Director, Motor Learning Laboratory,
Division of Health, Physical Education and Recreation,
The University of Toledo, Toledo, Ohio

Illustrations by JoAnne Royston

Lea & Febiger *1971 • Philadelphia*

Health Education, Physical Education,
and Recreational Series

RUTH ABERNATHY, Ph.D., EDITORIAL ADVISER

Director, School of Physical and Health Education,
University of Washington, Seattle, Washington 98105

ISBN 0-8121-0359-9

Library of Congress Catalog Card Number: 70-157467

Published in Great Britain by Henry Kimpton Publishers, London
Printed in the United States of America

Dedicated to
Kara Louise

FOREWORD

The great concern of Americans for education and educational change is more often represented by lip service than by actual, innovative action programs. Even more unfortunate is the fact that this condition pertains so often to the field of education for the mentally retarded. There are relatively few countries in the world today, with Israel a notable exception, where substantial educational concerns, efforts, and funds are directed toward helping handicapped children. As Professor Drowatzky has so aptly stated in the first sentence of his preface, "The education of mentally retarded individuals has frequently represented little more than baby sitting."

Professor Drowatzky has not written a book for teachers of the mentally retarded who can do little more than act as baby sitters. Instead, he has first made a complete analysis of the nature of mental retardation, the relationship between perceptual-motor training and other aspects of education, and the type of perceptual-motor skills most needed in an effective program for mental retardates. He has then gone further and provided the teacher of mentally retarded children with the basic professional information and methodology he needs to plan activity programs for the handicapped child. This book is a careful blending of theoretical orientation to the subject and practical know-how concerning specific activities and teaching techniques.

Physical activities greatly help children to learn about themselves. It has been suggested by some that much of our learning in the cognitive, affective, and motor skills domains is directly dependent upon early locomotor and manipulative experiences. This book clearly develops this trend of thinking and suggests that these experiences be included in educational programs for the mentally retarded. Professor Drowatzky develops this theme clearly and directly. This book is for anyone who wants to increase the learning possibilities for mentally retarded children and help them achieve success in the world they face.

George E. Dickson, Dean,
College of Education,
The University of Toledo

PREFACE

In the past, the education of mentally retarded individuals has frequently represented little more than baby sitting. Although general developments in special education have produced teachers and programs that help these children to more nearly reach their potential and engage in more productive lives, not all phases of education have reached such a state simultaneously.

For a number of years, physical education programs for these children have been poorly planned and were taught most often by teachers who were not physical education specialists. Therefore, the most frequent approach to the physical education of these children consisted of various low organized games and similar activities.

This book approaches the problem through two methods. First, the material is simplified and presented so that the special teacher of mentally retarded children who has little or no training in physical education will be able to use the material for instructional purposes. Although this is the primary audience for which the book was designed, this material also will be of use to the professional physical educator working in this area and to parents with the sincere desire to learn how to help their retarded child.

Second, a serious attempt has been made to integrate the theoretical framework for the selection of the activities with the presentation methods. I hope that this approach will enable the teacher to develop a better physical education program than would be possible if only activities were presented.

Physical Education for the Mentally Retarded would appear to be especially useful as (1) a desk copy for all classroom teachers, physical educators, and supervisors of programs for mentally retarded children; (2) a textbook in a class or workshop dealing with activity programs for special education teachers; (3) a textbook for classes conducted for physical education teachers, supervisors, or consultants; (4) a resource book for in-service training programs for classroom teachers; and (5) a source book for parents interested in working with their children.

ix

The book has been divided into two parts for convenient use. The first five chapters present the theoretical orientation of the book and deal with the nature and causes of mental retardation, the fitness and motor characteristics of retardates, and the learning process and planning of physical education programs for retarded children.

The last seven chapters are of a more practical nature. In these, specific activities and teaching techniques are presented for the improvement of physical fitness, basic movement skills, and perceptual-motor skills. Low organized games, lead-up activities, and sports and recreational skills are presented in Chapter 10. In Chapters 11 and 12, the reader is directed toward various teaching aids, special equipment, and other resources useful in teaching mentally retarded children.

I am indebted to the many people who have made this book possible. Among them are the retarded children with whom I have worked, the members of the Lucas County Association for Retarded Children, and the teachers in the LARC school and camp programs. Special thanks go to my wife Linnea, Dr. Albert Palmer, and Dr. Ruth Abernathy for their helpful suggestions and criticisms of the manuscript.

Toledo, Ohio   *John N. Drowatzky,* Ed.D.

CONTENTS

CHAPTER 1

Introduction

The term "mental retardation" is used in an attempt to classify a particular group of handicapped persons. These people are by no means homogeneous in behavior, intellectual function, physical characteristics or abilities, developmental levels, or other pertinent characteristics. For many years a person labeled as mentally retarded was considered to have an uncertain future, and the education he received reflected this attitude.

Our educational practices have changed, however, with increased knowledge and the development of an understanding of mental retardation. Today the treatment of mental retardation is approached on a multi-disciplinary basis; the contributions of medical specialists, educators, occupational therapists, social workers, and other professionals are combined into extensive programs for those classified as mentally retarded.

The development of specialized physical education programs for the mentally retarded is a relatively recent occurrence, and has been accompanied by the preparation of competent instructors. Among the factors contributing to the development of physical education programs for the retarded are changes associated with education, an understanding of the importance of physical activity, and the growth of agencies interested in the problems of the retarded. A brief discussion of each of these factors will serve to place the present development of the field into perspective.

EDUCATIONAL CHANGES

For many years the education of the mentally retarded was relegated to special schools which were physically separated from the public schools and whose functions were mainly custodial. In recent years, however, parents of retarded children requested that the public schools admit their children too, a request that was honored because these parents also pay taxes to support the public school system. The federal government provided additional funds for the support of educational programs involving students with various difficulties; projects to train teachers in special education were able to increase both their scope and enrollment.

A similar development took place in physical education. Elementary school programs were established under the direction of specially prepared teachers, who often came in contact with retarded children. In order to meet the retardate's special needs, physical education programs were adapted for handicapped children and educators with this interest received special training. Other teachers learned about activities for the retarded in workshops conducted by physical education instructors experienced in working with the handicapped child.

IMPORTANCE OF PHYSICAL ACTIVITY

Physical activity is an important factor in the learning process; it makes objects available to the child and enables him to learn about himself. Once the child learns the locomotor patterns of walking or running, he is able to explore his environment and develop the concept of space; he learns the relationships of objects to other objects and to himself. He is able to explore the characteristics of objects by manipulating them and develops concepts of their characteristics. Some researchers have suggested that all learning, academic as well as motor, is dependent upon the early locomotor and manipulative experiences.

Physical activities also enable the child to learn about himself. This knowledge is called body image and reflects the awareness that a child has about his characteristics, what he can do with his body, how much space it requires, and the like. Body image is believed to be both an aspect of the personality and an influence on the child's behavior. Successful experience in physical activity is believed to enhance the development of a favorable body image, while sparse or unsuccessful experience contributes to the formation of a poor body image.

AGENCIES

A number of groups interested in the problems of the handicapped were formed during and after the 1940's. The *National Association for Retarded Children*, organized in 1940, has become a powerful lobby force for the mentally retarded. Most of the members of this organization are parents, but teachers and other interested persons frequently participate. This group also functions at the state and county level in many regions of the country. At the local level, members of the Association often assist in school programs and sponsor other activities for retarded children. An example of this is Camp Courage, a residential summer camp sponsored by the Lucas County, (Ohio) Association for Retarded Children. Members of LARC are active in most phases of the camp operation, planning, and development. Other parents' groups assist school personnel with projects that enhance their teaching of the retarded and provide auxiliary services.

The *President's Panel on Mental Retardation is composed of well-qualified* persons who make recommendations concerning the problems of the mentally retarded. The major goal of the Panel is to enable each individual to achieve as much of his potential as possible. The areas of urgent concern have been enrichment learning for preschool children, development of instructional materials, improvement in state and local leadership, establishment of specialized classrooms, improved services in educational and psychological diagnosis, and evaluation for early detection of retardation. That these goals have not been met is due largely to financial limitations and the lack of qualified teachers.

In the 1950's, the *Joseph P. Kennedy, Jr., Foundation* was established to search for ways to prevent and eliminate retardation in the United States. The Kennedy Foundation works toward this goal by financing medical research, educational research and training, and rehabilitative research and training in the field of retardation. Physical education and recreation programs have been supported by the Kennedy Foundation in a number of ways. It has conducted workshops, financed research, supported camp programs, developed a special Olympics program to encourage sports participation by the retarded, and disseminated information about physical education and recreation programs for the retarded. In addition, the Foundation has developed a physical fitness test and award program in cooperation with the *American Association for Health, Physical Education and Recreation (AAHPER)*.

Additional programs of physical education and recreation for the mentally retarded which were developed by AAHPER, stimulated the cooperation of other agencies, such as the Kennedy Foundation mentioned previously. In addition to the physical fitness test and award program, the AAHPER publishes materials concerning activities for the retarded, compiles information about the funding of physical education and research, and communicates information about current programs, research developments, and resources relating to physical education and recreation programs for the retarded.

FUNCTIONAL EDUCATION

Due to the influences of the various associations and the increased involvement of concerned educators, today's education for the retarded is concerned with functional and adaptive behavior, and attempts to correct the various behavioral deficiencies that are observed in these children. Thus, all materials and programs for the retarded must be concerned with the further development of self-help and occupational skills. Attainment of these goals usually requires that complex skills be analyzed and subdivided into simple skills which are then taught and recombined in many ways.

Educational programs for the mentally retarded revolve about the improvement of the child's performance and functional abilities. Broad in scope and encompassing many disciplines, each makes its unique contribution by encouraging the child to perform adequately within his social, personal, and occupational environment.

Physical education is a vital part of the educational program, contributing greatly to the child's perceptual-motor skill development. Motor patterns developed and improved through physical education contribute greatly to the child's success in his social, personal, and occupational encounters. It is to these goals that the program described in this book is aimed, for the skills described here can aid the retarded child to realize a more productive and satisfying life.

CHAPTER 2

The Nature of Mental Retardation

The classification of mentally retarded individuals is not a modern development; a great deal of the work in this field was done in France during the first half of the 19th century. Most of the early attempts to identify mentally deficient individuals centered about the observation of various physical measures, especially the size and formation of the skull. The present system used to classify mental abilities is based on work of the early 1900's by Alfred Binet, who was commissioned by the French Minister of Public Instruction to develop a device that would locate children unable to profit from normal education.

The first intelligence scale, the 1905 Binet-Simon scale, was constructed as an answer to this problem. This "intelligence" test developed the fundamental concept employed in all tests used to measure mental abilities: that is, differences in mental development may be identified by looking at divergencies from the average mental abilities of children of various ages. Thus, since Binet's original contribution, individual differences in mental ability have been determined through the use of standardized tests.

As a consequence of the use and development of standardized mental tests, many psychologists, educators, and other interested persons began to debate the nature of the condition described as mental retardation. "Is mental retardation a permanent condition? Should social incompetence be considered as a factor in retardation? Does mental retardation represent an inability to adapt to the 'normal environment' of one's fellows?"

A historical survey of mental retardation indicates that most early definitions included the concepts of incurability and a constitutional origin. Furthermore, many early definitions used either scores on an intelligence test or social functioning alone as the sole criterion for determining mental retardation. These definitions soon became inadequate, and in 1959 the American Association on Mental Deficiency adopted the following definition:

Mental retardation refers to subaverage general intellectual functioning which originates during the developmental period and is associated with impairment in adaptive behavior.... Furthermore an individual may meet the criteria of mental retardation at one time and not at another. A person may change status as a result of changes in social standards or conditions or as a result of changes in efficiency of intellectual functioning, with level of efficiency always being determined in relation to the behavioral standards and norms for the individuals' chronological age group. (Heber, 1959, pp. 3—4.)

Mental retardation is thus defined as a reversible condition that reflects an individual's current status based upon his intellectual functioning and adaptive behavior. In contrast to previous definitions, it is now recognized that changes in an individual's status are possible. These changes may be due to a change in social standards, technology, environmental conditions such as leaving school, or a difference in the efficiency of intellectual functioning.

CLASSIFICATION OF RETARDATION

Inasmuch as the problem of mental retardation involves many professions, various terms have been developed to describe differing degrees of retardation. The professional groups concerned with systems of classification include educational and psychiatric legal bodies, as well as the American Association on Mental Deficiency (AAMD), which encompasses many different professions. The varied interests of these groups have led to the development of systems appropriate to their specific needs but differing in terminology and classification levels. The general schemes of classification used by these agencies and described by scores on intelligence tests are presented in Table 2—1.

Table 2—1.   Comparison of Mental Retardation Classification Schemes

AAMD	Intelligence Quotient	Educational	Psychiatric/Legal
BORDERLINE RETARDATION (85, 75)	90, 80, 70	BORDERLINE OR SLOW LEARNER	
MILD RETARDATION (65, 55)	60	EDUCABLE MENTALLY RETARDED	MORON
MODERATE RETARDATION (45, 35)	50, 40	TRAINABLE MENTALLY RETARDED	
SEVERE RETARDATION (25)	30, 20		IMBECILE
PROFOUND RETARDATION (15, 5)	10, 0	DEPENDENT MENTALLY RETARDED	IDIOT

The psychiatric classification system was developed earlier than either of the other systems and was adopted for use by the legal-administrative profession. Because of the stigma attached to these terms and a need for more definitive classifications, the educational and AAMD systems evolved. Frequently, the intelligence quotient level qualifying as retardation and the critical level of retardation needed for governmental support varies from state to state. Probably the best system of classification available today is that proposed by the American Association on Mental Deficiency. This system emphasizes the current level of the individual's functioning and views classification as an ongoing process. It attempts to classify individuals in this system according to measurements of both intellectual functioning and adaptive behavior.

Adaptive Behavior

The measurement of intellectual function by objective intelligence tests is better known than the concept of adaptive behavior. However, the concept of adaptive behavior facilitates a more realistic evaluation of the individual as he relates to the natural and social demands of his surroundings because it refers to the appropriateness with which an individual responds to his environment. Adaptive behavior has two major aspects: the degree to which a person is able to function independently and his ability to meet the culturally imposed demands of personal and social responsibility. Adaptive behavior is a composite of many aspects of behavior and depends upon a wide range of specific abilities and disabilities. Thus, a complete evaluation of an individual's level of function must take into consideration his social, emotional, self-help, motivational, perceptual-motor, recreational, occupational, and safety abilities.

High levels of functioning require that an individual be able to generalize his basic motor patterns to many different situations; consequently objective measures of adaptive behavior are, for the most part, unavailable. Check lists have been developed, however, to facilitate evaluation of certain aspects of adaptive behavior. An example is the Vineland Social Maturity Scale (Doll, 1953), a tool for the evaluation of motor, social, and linguistic aspects of development. The Social Maturity Scale focuses attention on the everyday activities of the individual in order to help the examiner obtain a more comprehensive picture of the subject's functioning. Norms are available from infancy through adulthood. The Vineland Social Maturity Scale is briefly described in Table 2.2.

The following description of a sheltered workshop situation will emphasize the importance of basic motor patterns in an occupational setting. The task in this situation is the packaging of different units into various kits. This operation requires several persons working at each of three stations. At the first station the items are counted, placed on small pallets, and transported on a manual conveyer to the packaging station. At the packaging stations the units

Table 2—2. Representative Items in Vineland Social Maturity Scale

Category	Approximate Age
General self-help items	
Rolls over	4 mo.
Stands alone	9 mo.
Overcomes simple obstacles	1 yr. 4 mo.
Asks to go to toilet	2 yrs.
Avoids simple hazards	2 yrs. 9 mo.
Cares for self at toilet	3 yrs. 10 mo.
Tells time to quarter hour	7 yrs. 4 mo.
Self-direction items	
Trusted with money	5 yrs. 9 mo.
Makes minor purchases	9 yrs. 5 mo.
Is left to care for self or others	11 yrs. 6 mo.
Goes out unsupervised in the daytime	16 yrs. 2 mo.
Assumes personal responsibility	20 yrs. 6 mo.
Locomotion items	
Walks around room unattended	1 yr. 1 mo.
Goes about house or yard	1 yr. 7 mo.
Walks upstairs unassisted	1 yr. 8 mo.
Walks downstairs one step per tread	3 yrs. 3 mo.
Goes around neighborhood unattended	4 yrs. 8 mo.
Goes to school unattended	5 yrs. 10 mo.
Goes about town freely	9 yrs. 6 mo.
Socialization	
Reaches for familiar persons	4 mo.
Plays with other children	1 yr. 6 mo.
Plays cooperatively at kindergarten level	3 yrs. 3 mo.
Plays competitive exercise games	5 yrs. 2 mo.
Plays simple table games	5 yrs. 7 mo.
Participates in pre-adolescent play	8 yrs. 3 mo.
Plays difficult games	12 yrs. 4 mo.

From Doll, 1953.

are lifted from the pallets, placed into bags with assembly instructions, the bags are then tied and placed on a moving conveyer belt. At the final station, the completed packages are picked from the moving belt and placed into a box. When the boxes are filled, they are closed, prepared for shipping, and then taken to the shipping station on a hand truck.

Analysis of this packaging job reveals several motor patterns. The person working at the first station must be able to *move* in an efficient locomotor pattern; *carry* the objects to the sorting station; *grasp, lift,* and *manipulate* the units to be packaged; *release* and *stack* the objects on the pallets; and *push* the loaded pallets to the packing stations. The packing station requires workers who are able to *grasp* and *lift* the units from the pallets, *carry* them from the pallets to the bags, *manipulate* them into the bags, and *tie* the bags and *place* them onto a moving conveyer belt. The final station requires that the completed packages are *grasped* and *lifted* from the moving conveyer, *placed* into a shipping box; the box is then *manipulated* and closed; closed boxes are *lifted* onto a hand truck and the hand truck is *pushed* into the shipping station.

The importance of motor patterns in adaptive behavior, especially in occupational settings, is evident from this task description. Motor patterns were mentioned some 20 times during the packing operation. If any one of the required motor patterns is missing, if the person cannot make the required perceptual-motor adjustments, or if he does not have the strength to lift the items, then he will be unable to function in such a setting. The use of effective motor patterns and perceptual-motor operations is no less important in other areas of adaptive behavior which require self-help, recreational, social, and safety skills. Thus, if a mental retardate lacks the ability to apply appropriate motor patterns to the situations he encounters, his level of functioning is greatly reduced. Table 2–3 summarizes the levels of adaptive behavior that have been generally associated with different degrees of retardation.

While the levels of intellectual functioning and adaptive behavior describe the person's present state, more knowledge about the retarded individual is usually required before his entry into any training program. Most institutions evaluate the applicant prior to initiation of training and may seek to determine the cause of his mental retardation. This information, combined with the knowledge of his present status, may provide important clues for both the development of a training program and the prognosis for future development.

CAUSES OF RETARDATION

Because of its complex nature, mental retardation does not fit into any simple pattern of definition or classification. Thus we cannot treat mentally retarded children as a homogeneous group, even when they are grouped according to intellectual ability as previously described in this chapter. In spite of the fact that certain characteristics are frequently associated with degrees of mental retardation, the cause, effect, and treatment differ widely among individuals. Consequently, each individualized program in physical education, special education, or occupational training for the retardate is based on all available information about his condition.

Today it is recognized that mental retardation is not a disease; rather, it is a condition that may or may not be caused by disease. The condition of mental retardation may occur during the development of the fetus, during the birth process, shortly after birth, or during the child's early growth and development period. The problem is further complicated by the fact that its

Table 2—3.   **Levels of Adaptive Behavior**

Degrees Of Retardation	Pre-School Age (0—5 Years) Maturation and Development	School Age (6—21 Years) Training and Education	Adult (Over 21 Years) Social and Vocational Adequacy
Mild	Can develop social and communication skills; minimal retardation in sensorimotor areas; rarely distinguished from normal until later age.	Can learn academic skills to approximately 6th-grade level by late teens. Cannot learn general high school subjects. Needs special education particularly at secondary school age. levels. ("Educable.")	Capable of social and vocational adequacy with proper education and training. Frequently needs supervision and guidance under serious social or economic stress.
Moderate	Can talk or learn to communicate; peer social awareness; fair motor development; may profit from self-help; can be managed with moderate supervision.	Can learn functional academic skills to approximately 4th-grade level by late teens if given special education. ("Educable.")	Capable of self-maintenance in unskilled or semi-skilled occupations; needs supervision and guidance when under mild social or economic stress.
Severe	Poor motor development; speech is minimal; generally unable to profit from training in self-help; little or no communication skills.	Can talk or learn to communicate; can be trained in elemental health habits; cannot learn functional academic skills; profits from systematic habit training. ("Trainable.")	Can contribute partially to self-support under complete supervision; can develop self-protection skills to a minimal useful level in controlled environment.
Profound	Gross retardation; minimal capacity for functioning in sensorimotor areas; needs nursing care.	Some motor development present; cannot profit from training in self-help; needs total care. ("Dependent.")	Some motor and speech development; totally incapable of self-maintenance; needs complete care and supervision.

From *An Introduction to Mental Retardation,* 1965, p. 3.

cause may be accurately diagnosed in only 15 to 25% of the cases. In an attempt to remove some of the confusion surrounding the causes of retardation, specialists have developed a system of classification, congruent with the concepts of modern medicine and rehabilitation, which may be used by all who are concerned with the problem of mental retardation. This system of terminology and classification was consequently adopted by the American Association on Mental Deficiency (Heber, 1959). It describes eight major groups with a series of subgroups in each of the broad categories. It also notes the period of development during which mental retardation originates and the degree of central nervous system involvement. This *Medical Classification* system is briefly outlined in Table 2—4.

It is also possible to categorize retardation broadly as organic or endogenous (brain-damaged) and non-organic or exogenous. In the *Medical Classification*, the first seven categories would fall under the heading of endogenous or brain damage, while the last category would represent the exogenous or non-organically retarded. In terms of relative incidence, approximately 85 to 90% of retarded individuals would be included under the eighth category. Furthermore, in terms of severity, the majority of the retarded would be characterized as educable or mildly retarded persons; it has been estimated that between 75 to 90% of the subjects are mildly retarded. Regardless of the degree of severity, perceptual disturbances, thinking disorders, behavioral disorders, and various motor disturbances appear to be more prevalent among children in whom the diagnosis of some brain damage is made. Thus, program development must take into account both the degree of severity and the causal agents.

INCIDENCE OF MENTAL RETARDATION

The incidence of mental retardation depends upon the nature of the population being evaluated and the criteria used to classify the individual as retarded. Perhaps the most important factor in determining the functional level of individuals described as mentally retarded is the socio-economic and cultural level of the community. In societies requiring high degrees of training, more individuals may be classified as retarded than in societies requiring less training. This is evident in our present society, where the number classified as retarded rises greatly during the school years and decreases afterwards, suggesting that persons who have difficulty in coping with the demands of the academic setting may have little or no difficulty in sustaining themselves after school. As technological levels rise, mental retardation may well become an increasingly important problem for society, especially in dealing with those individuals having only slight impairments in functioning.

The socio-economic and cultural levels of the community affect the incidence of mental retardation in still another way. Children growing up in low

Table 2—4. Outline of Medical Classification of Mental Deficiency

I.   *Diseases and conditions due to infection.* This category includes maternal diseases such as syphilis, encephalitis, and German measles during pregnancy; and postnatal infections accompanying measles, whooping cough, scarlet fever, encephalitis, meningitis, and other childhood diseases known to cause brain damage.

II. *Diseases and conditions due to intoxication.* Prenatal conditions such as toxemia of pregnancy and blood incompatibility (Rh factor) and postnatal intoxicating substances, poisons, and various drugs that cause nervous tissue injury are among the agents included in this topic.

III. *Diseases and conditions due to trauma or physical agent.* Included as causal agents are injuries that occur during the prenatal stage as a result of irradiation or of oxygen deprivation due to maternal asphyxia, maternal anemia or hypotension and birth injuries that are caused by complications during delivery and lack of oxygen during the birth process; older children may suffer physical injury to the nervous system by near-suffocation, automobile accidents and the like.

IV. *Diseases and conditions due to disorder of metabolism, growth or nutrition.* This category includes inborn metabolic disorders such as phenylketonuria (PKU) as well as pre- and postnatal nutritional deprivation that inhibits nervous system development.

V.   *Diseases and conditions due to new growths.* Various hereditary tumors and growths of the central nervous system having variable expressions may cause mental retardation. These conditions may or may not be progressive.

VI. *Diseases and conditions due to (unknown) prenatal influence.* Among the types of mental retardation commonly included in this classification are various cerebral defects such as absence of the brain, primary cranial anomalies (i.e., hydrocephaly, or microcephaly), and Down's syndrome or mongolism.*

VII. *Diseases and conditions due to unknown or uncertain cause with structural reactions manifest.* Mental retardation resulting from excessive growth of connective tissue in the central nervous system, degeneration of the cerebellum and conditions resulting from prematurity are included in this grouping.

VIII. *Due to uncertain (or presumed psychologic) cause with functional reactions alone manifest.* This category includes mental retardation with no apparent organic defect, believed to be caused by cultural-familial, environmental deprivation, emotional, psychotic. or other factors.

*Although mongolism is listed under unknown prenatal influences in this system, the cause of the condition was located in 1959. The mongoloid child is known to possess 47 chromosomes instead of the usual 46. The condition occurs most frequently when the mother is over 35 years of age.

From Heber, 1959.

socio-economic and cultural settings are more likely to suffer from the effects of deprivation. If the child has not had the experiences necessary for the intellectual growth that society deems important, he is likely to be classified as mentally retarded. This relationship between the socio-economic status of a community and the rate of retardation among school age children is well summarized in Table 2—5.

Table 2—5. Estimated Rate of Retardation per 1000 School-Age Children

Level of Community	Totally Dependent	Trainable	Educable	Slow Learner
Low	1	4	50	300
Middle	1	4	25	170
High	1	4	10	50

From Kirk, 1962.

Table 2—5 emphasizes the differences in the number of educable and slow learning children supported by low, middle, and high socio-economic areas. According to Kirk (1962), these data indicate that pathological conditions, such as mongolism, occur at the same frequency regardless of the socio-economic and cultural level of the family. This table does not indicate the larger population that would be classified as mentally retarded during school age years compared to ages either before entry into school or after termination of education. However, the majority of children classified as slow learners and many educable retarded children would be included in this category. It is clear that incidence will vary greatly with both the populations involved and the criteria used to judge impaired mental functioning.

SUMMARY

The definition of mental retardation has undergone many changes during the past half century. In 1959, the American Association on Mental Deficiency defined mental retardation as "subaverage intellectual functioning which originates during the developmental period and is associated with impairment in adaptive behavior." This definition does not consider mental retardation as either incurable or as a result of only constitutional factors. The concept of adaptive behavior considers social and behavioral standards as well as intellectual criteria. Several other classification systems have been developed to meet various legal, medical, or educational requirements.

The most common tool used to detect mentally retarded children has been the intelligence test. The modern concept of retardation also requires the evaluation of the affective-emotional, motivational, social, and perceptual-motor skills of the individual. The program developed for mentally retarded individuals must be individual in nature and must be based on an evaluation of both the degree of severity and cause of the condition.

The incidence of mental retardation varies greatly, being affected by the nature of the community being evaluated and the tools used to detect the deficiency. The educable, or mildly retarded, and slow learner categories are most influenced by the socio-economic and cultural levels of the community.

REFERENCES

An Introduction to Mental Retardation. U. S. Department of Health, Education and Welfare, Secretary's Committee on Mental Retardation, Washington, D.C., 1965.

Doll, Edgar A.: *The Measurement of Social Competence.* Educational Test Bureau, 1953.

Heber, R. (Ed.): A manual on terminology and classification in mental retardation. *Monogr. Suppl., Amer J. Ment. Defic.* 64, No. 2, 1959.

Kirk, Samuel A.: *Educating Exceptional Children.* Boston: Houghton Mifflin Company, 1962.

CHAPTER 3

Fitness and Motor Characteristics

Two factors emerge from a review of research that has been conducted into the physical education of mentally retarded children. First, many systems of classification have been developed, but no one system appears to be completely satisfactory. This may be due to the fact that no two mentally retarded children are identical and a large number of conditions exhibited by them may be either causal or concomitant. Often it is impossible to determine which is the case in conditions such as congenital malformations, prematurity, epilepsy, cerebral palsy, deafness, and multiple handicaps.

Second, faced with these seemingly insurmountable problems, investigators have apparently declined to pursue research directed toward program development. Experimental studies of comparative educational techniques for the handicapped are almost nonexistent. Several years ago, for example, Beck (1956) reported that none of the Illinois school districts providing physical education programs for mentally retarded children were carrying on research in this area of special education. Furthermore, the objective of preparing children to use their spare time in a socially acceptable manner was completely ignored. Recent reports by Brace (1966, 1967) suggested that this situation may not have improved to any great extent. These surveys indicated the principal needs of physical education programs for mentally retarded children to be: (a) teachers with adequate preparation; (b) instruction in recreational skills; (c) adequate facilities; and (d) continued instruction for teachers of mentally retarded children. A further discussion of related needs was also included in these reports, but no mention was made of continuing research assessing the results of on-going programs.

In view of these findings, the purpose of this chapter is to present brief summaries of research that are pertinent to the evaluation of physical education for mentally retarded children. Studies dealing with body weight, physical fitness, motor ability, and the effect of programs for the retarded will be discussed.

15

BODY WEIGHT

One problem recognized by many persons concerned with the treatment and training of mentally retarded children has been that of weight control. Benda (1960) stated that a reliable early symptom of mongolism is the condition of general bodily hypotonia or flabbiness with excessive distributions of fat in the abdominal and breast areas. This tendency toward overweight is relative to body size; as mongoloids are often shorter in stature than the average person of their age, their weight may appear to be within the normal range for that age. When their weight is compared with their actual height, however, mongoloids are often as much as 10 to 30 pounds overweight.

Culley and others (1963) investigated the heights, weights, and body builds of a population of institutionalized mentally retarded children. Their findings supported Benda's statement about body size, and further suggested that mentally retarded patients without motor dysfunction were similar to mongoloids in terms of body measures.

PHYSICAL FITNESS

The general condition of hypotonia, or flabbiness, has also been indirectly supported by the results of studies of the physical fitness of mentally retarded individuals. Several studies have indicated that mentally retarded children, as a general rule, achieve below the normal children on tests of physical fitness. When the Kraus-Weber test of minimum muscular fitness was administered to 72 female trainable mentally retarded subjects, Drowatzky (1967) observed that 90% of these subjects were not able to pass the test battery. Most of these failures were multiple failures. In a second study using male subjects, this investigator (Drowatzky, 1968) observed that 72% of the trainable mentally retarded subjects were unable to pass this test of minimal fitness; 62% experienced multiple failures. Brown (1967) reported that approximately 79% of his sample of trainable mentally retarded children were unable to pass the Kraus-Weber test with 63% experiencing multiple failures. The results of these studies are given in Figure 3–1.

Sengstock (1966) compared American Association for Health, Physical Education, and Recreation Physical Fitness Test item scores of educable mentally retarded children with those obtained by normal children of either the same chronological age or the same mental age (Table 3–1). His results indicated that the EMR children achieved lower scores than normal children of the same chronological age and achieved higher scores for several items than normal children the same mental age who were younger chronologically. Thus, these mentally retarded children generally achieved relatively low physical fitness scores on standard test batteries when compared with normals of the same physical age. In a study comparing a group of intellectually normal children with three groups of educable mentally retarded boys, Auxter (1961) also reported lower achievement among EMR children. The

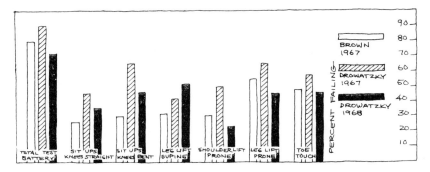

Figure 3—1. Comparison of Kraus-Weber test item failure rates observed in trainable retarded children.

Table 3—1.   Comparison of Educable Mentally Retarded and Normal Children on AAHPER Physical Fitness Test Items

Test Items	Mean Scores		
Pull-ups (trials)	1.73	1.60	2.87
Sit-ups (trials)	37.13	37.83	58.53
Shuttle run (seconds)	12.16	12.79	11.11
Standing broad jump (inches)	57.23	49.80	67.27
50-Yard dash (seconds)	8.38	9.15	7.87
Softball throw (feet)	99.13	70.33	130.07
600-Yard run-walk (minutes and seconds)	2:41	2:56	2:22
	EMR	Normal Same MA	Normal Same CA
Chronological age (months)	158.83	111.47	158.60
Mental age (months)	114.40	114.13	157.80
Intelligence quotient	72.13	102.73	99.53
Height (inches)	59.67	52.47	61.63
Weight (pounds)	98.10	66.20	107.53

From Sengstock, 1966.

normal children were observed to be significantly superior to the retarded boys on the vertical jump, grip strength, and ankle flexibility measures. Further, Auxter's nonorganically retarded subjects scored better than the organically and undifferentiated retarded groups on the vertical jump test (Fig. 3—2). This difference might be attributed to the fact that nonorganically retarded children have less deficiency in perceptual-motor skill learning than children with brain damage.

The results of these fitness studies have indicated that large numbers of trainable retarded children were unable to pass tests of minimal muscular fitness and that educable retarded children are generally observed to score

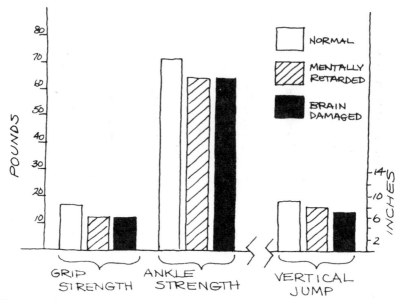

Figure 3–2. Comparison of selected strength and fitness measures of normal and educable mentally retarded children. (Data from Auxter, 1961.)

lower than normal children on tests of physical fitness and strength. Physical fitness activities may often constitute the foundation of the entire program. Many students enroll in the program with such low levels of strength and endurance that it is necessary to develop their physical fitness before they are able to participate meaningfully in a program of skills instruction. Evaluation of the initial status of each child becomes increasingly important in programs for retarded children; it provides the means for initial placement of the student and the determination of the program's effectiveness.

MOTOR SKILLS

Research has indicated that mentally retarded children also achieve lower scores than normal children on tests of general motor skills. When data gathered by Francis and Rarick (1959) dealing with the motor abilities of retarded children were compared with data obtained from normal children, the retarded children exhibited consistently inferior performances in grip strength, shoulder girdle strength, speed of running, standing broad jump, vertical jump, soft-ball throw for distance, squat thrusts, and reaction time. These comparisons are summarized in Figures 3–3 through 3–10. Note that in many instances both the normal boys and girls achieved superior scores to both groups of retarded children.

Various other studies (Malpass, 1963; Cratty, 1967; Greenfell, 1965; Rarick, 1967; Sengstock, 1966; Stevens and Heber, 1964) have also indicated

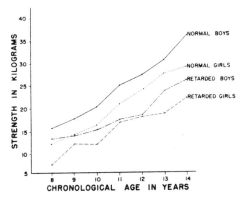

Figure 3—3. Mean strength of right grip for normal and mentally retarded boys and girls. [Data on normal boys and girls adapted from Meredith (1935), Metheny (1941), and Jones by Francis and Rarick (1959). Data for retarded boys and girls from Francis and Rarick (1959).] (From Francis and Rarick: *Amer. J. Ment. Defic.* 63:803, 1959. Reprint by permission from the *American Journal of Mental Deficiency.* Copyright 1959, American Association on Mental Deficiency.)

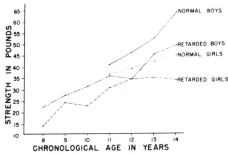

Figure 3—4. Mean shoulder girdle strength of normal and mentally retarded boys and girls: Pull. [Data on normal boys and girls adapted from Meredith (1935), Metheny (1941), and Jones (1949) by Francis and Rarick (1959). Data for retarded boys and girls from Francis and Rarick (1959).] (From Francis and Rarick: *Amer. J. Ment. Defic.* 63:804, 1959. Reprinted by permission from the *American Journal of Mental Deficiency.* Copyright 1959, American Association on Mental Deficiency.)

differences between the scores of normal and retarded children in motor ability parameters as measured by the Lincoln-Oseretsky Motor Development Scale and other standardized tests. Furthermore, some of these sources reported that significant relationships existed between the mental and motor ability scores of retardates.

Not only do differences exist in the motor skills of normal and retarded children, but differences also exist among retarded children of the same mental ability. Cratty (1967) reported that the child with mongolism is inferior, without exception, to other trainable retarded children; these latter

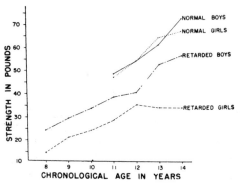

Figure 3—5. Mean shoulder girdle strength of normal and mentally retarded boys and girls: Thrust. [Data on normal boys and girls adapted from Jones (1949), Neilson and Cozens (1934), and Espenschade (1940) by Francis and Rarick (1959). Data for retarded boys and girls from Francis and Rarick (1959).] (From Francis and Rarick: *Amer. J. Ment. Defic.* 63:804, 1959. Reprinted by permission from the *American Journal of Mental Deficiency.* Copyright 1959, American Association on Mental Deficiency.)

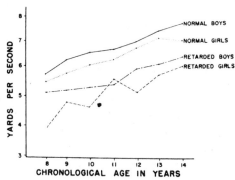

Figure 3—6. Speed-of-running data for normal and mentally retarded children by chronological age. [Data on normal boys and girls adapted from Jones (1949), Neilson and Cozens (1934), and Espenschade (1940) by Francis and Rarick (1959). Data for retarded boys and girls from Francis and Rarick (1959).] (From Francis and Rarick: *Amer. J. Ment. Defic.* 63:806, 1959. Reprinted by permission from the *American Journal of Mental Deficiency.* Copyright 1959, American Association on Mental Deficiency.)

children, in turn, are generally inferior to educable retarded children. Woodward and Stern (1963) reported that locomotor development is more advanced in retarded children than is sensorimotor or speech development; sensorimotor development precedes speech development. These authors

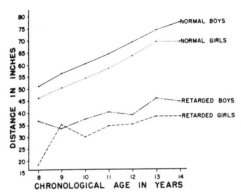

Figure 3—7. Comparison of mean performance scores in the standing broad jump for normal and mentally retarded children, by chronological age. [Data on normal boys and girls adapted from McCloy (1954) and Neilson and Cozens (1934) by Francis and Rarick (1959). Data for retarded boys and girls from Francis and Rarick (1959).] (From Francis and Rarick: *Amer. J. Ment. Defic.* 63:805, 1959. Reprinted by permission from the *American Journal of Mental Deficiency.* Copyright 1959, American Association on Mental Deficiency.)

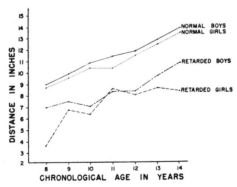

Figure 3—8. Comparison of mean performance scores in vertical jump for normal and mentally retarded children, by chronological age. (From Francis and Rarick: *Amer. J. Ment. Defic.* 63:805, 1959. Reprinted by permission from the *American Journal of Mental Deficiency.* Copyright 1959, American Association on Mental Deficiency.)

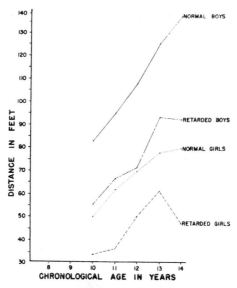

Figure 3—9. Comparison of mean performance scores of the softball throw for distance for normal and mentally retarded children, by chronological age. (From Francis and Rarick: *Amer. J. Ment. Defic.* 63:806, 1959. Reprinted by permission from the *American Journal of Mental Deficiency.* Copyright 1959, American Association on Mental Deficiency.)

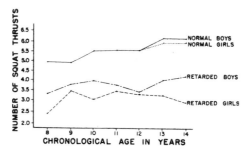

Figure 3—10. Comparison of mean performance scores on the Burpee squat-thrust test for normal and mentally retarded children, by chronological age. (From Francis and Rarick: *Amer. J. Ment. Defic.* 63:807, 1959. Reprinted by permission from the *American Journal of Mental Deficiency.* Copyright 1959, American Association on Mental Deficiency.)

attributed this pattern of development to maturational influences and suggested that severely subnormal children develop more rapidly in the maturational aspects, but more slowly in aspects that are dependent upon learning. In a study comparing motor skills of mentally retarded and normal children, Howe (1959) discovered that normal children were consistently superior to the mentally retarded children. Furthermore, the retarded children experienced particular difficulty in motor skills involving balance. The summary of research compiled by Malpass (1963) indicated that the discrepancies observed between normal and retarded children tended to increase with advancing age; this tendency was most marked for the more complex skills.

To summarize this research, it appears that retarded children are usually inferior to normal children in motor skill development. Differences in motor skill abilities are also observed in children with varying degrees of retardation. Two factors appear to be particularly important when considering the extent of the difference: the more severely retarded children appear to have consistently lower performance and, in complex tasks which require more learning the disparity between the performances of retarded and normal children is increased. Thus, motor skill instruction should be included as a basic element of the physical education program. The children appear to need assistance in the development of the basic movement skills such as running, jumping, catching, hopping, and the like. Once these elementary skills have been mastered, they can be combined and refined into the more advanced gross motor skills of striking a ball with a bat, running and kicking a ball, running and throwing a ball, and moving about while hopping on one foot. In any event, strong emphasis upon fundamental skill instruction and the improvement of skill levels appears to be an important ingredient of the physical education program for retarded children.

LEARNING PATTERNS

The perceptual-motor learning patterns of retarded individuals must be discussed cautiously. Inasmuch as no general factor has been located that would account for the differences observed in various learning tasks, these next few paragraphs must be interpreted with this cautionary note in mind.

According to summaries of studies by Denny (1964) and Lipman (1963), some completed research has indicated that reflexive types of learning are more difficult to establish in retarded subjects than in normal subjects. Other investigators, however, have reported no such differences between these groups of subjects. Most researchers agree that differences in the ability to learn conditioned reflexes apparently exist between organically and nonorganically retarded subjects. Moreover, there is general agreement that inhibition is impaired in retarded subjects, extinction is retarded, discrimination learning is poor, and delayed responses to stimuli are difficult to establish. In addition, the retarded child appears to be greatly affected by extraneous stimuli.

Denny and Lipman further reported that even the most severely retarded individuals are capable of some degree of learning, such as lifting an arm in response to a stimulus. As a general rule, however, the less severe the degree of retardation, the quicker the person will learn perceptual-motor tasks. Again, the majority of studies indicated that motor skill learning in normal children was superior to that of retarded children. The retarded individuals appear to have particular difficulty with some forms of discrimination learning, learning responses that depended upon verbal assistance, and focusing attention upon the relevant parts of a stimulus situation.

Some evidence suggests that the learning pattern of retarded individuals differs from that of normals. Heebøll-Nielsen (1967) reported that retarded subjects appear to progress differently from normal persons during a perceptual-motor skill training period and that the retardates experienced particular difficulties at the beginning of a training period. They found a daily "warming-up" period was necessary to overcome the retarded subjects' rigidity. Regardless of their learning differences, all but the most severely retarded can learn how to solve a series of related problems. The speed of acquisition, according to Denny (1964), appears to be directly related to mental age (Fig. 3–11); problem-solving performance of retardates is below that of normals and in the most severely retarded, it appears to be purely trial and error.

The reports of Denny (1964), Lipman (1963), and Heebøll-Neilsen (1967) all emphasized the fact that the retarded children's performance is initially lower on skilled motor tasks than that of normal children, but the retarded child will improve more rapidly, relatively, than the normal subject with practice, and, depending upon the skill, sometimes catch up with their performance. The most important characteristic of the motor task influencing the retardates' performance is its complexity; as the difficulty of the task increases, the importance of intelligence increases, and, despite relatively faster improvement, the retarded are unable to eliminate the difference existing between their performance and that of normal children.

ACTIVITY PROGRAMS FOR THE RETARDED

Few long-term physical education programs for mentally retarded children have been studied intensively, although several researchers have reported on programs of varying lengths. Perhaps the physical education program of longest duration to be evaluated was that conducted at the Institute of Logopedics in Wichita, Kansas. Established in 1962, this program was based on the orderly progression of physical fitness activities, basic skills instruction, and recreational activities. Drowatzky (1965) notes that the physical education program was originally developed for boys only, with instruction for girls instituted after the boys' program was well established. Improvement in the students' physical skills was evidenced by all ability groups, and the daily program of physical education produced significant gains in explosive power, muscular strength, agility, and endurance measures.

Other studies concerned with the effect of physical education programs

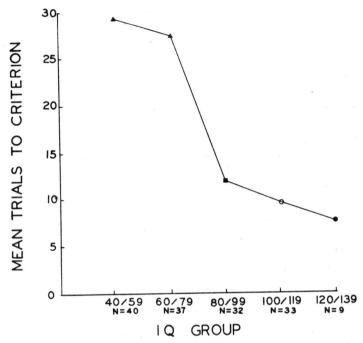

Figure 3—11. IQ and mean trials to criterion for retarded and normal subjects on a shielded-maze task. (From Ellis, Pryer, Distefano, and Pryer: *Amer. J. Ment. Defic.* 64:731, 1960. Reprinted by permission from *American Journal of Mental Deficiency.* Copyright 1960, American Association on Mental Deficiency.)

for mentally retarded children have also indicated that significant improvements in children's physical abilities can be realized. Howe (1959) compared familial mentally retarded boys and girls, aged 6 to 12 years, with normal children of the same chronological age on a series of motor skill tasks. In addition to observing that the normal children were superior on all motor tasks, he reported that the retardates had particular difficulty with balancing tasks and lacked realism in estimating how well they were succeeding in the tasks. Howe reported that the results of this study suggested that a structured program of physical education may be a necessary part of the curriculum for mentally retarded children.

Subjective evaluations of children's interest in physical activities and anecdotal records were used by Shotick and Thate (1960) to recommend the following procedures in physical education programs for mentally retarded children: (a) begin the program with simple activities that are generally competitive in nature; (b) select and emphasize activities that will hold the children's enthusiasm; (c) plan to include more than one activity during a physical education period; (d) emphasize explanation and demonstration of the rules and utilize play situations in the program; and, (e) move the children's bodies through the movement sequence whenever necessary to facilitate learning.

Greenfell (1965) reported the effects of a structured physical education program on the physical fitness and motor educability of educable mentally retarded children in primary school grades. These children, attending special education classes, participated in a 10-week physical education program and were then evaluated by the investigator. He reported that educable retarded children have the capacity to learn basic motor skills; their physical fitness can be improved and they are able to learn all of the same motor skills that normal children learn. Greenfell also found that the physical education program had beneficial effects on the retardates' social and intellectual growth.

A group of educationally subnormal boys were placed in a 10-week physical conditioning program by Oliver (1958). At the end of this time the group was compared with a group of similar students receiving the normal physical education program which consisted of two lessons each week plus organized games. Evaluation at the end of this program indicated significant improvement in both physical and mental abilities derived from participation in the physical conditioning program. The increase in physical abilities was attributed to participation in the activities of the program while the mental improvement was attributed to an improvement in the boys' motivational states.

The effects of participation in a physical education program upon certain aspects of intellectual, physical, and social development was investigated by Corder (1965). The students in this program received physical education training five days a week for four weeks. Among the findings reported by Corder were: (a) some changes on certain scales of the WISC Intelligence Test; (b) significant gains in the physical performance measures; and (c) no changes on the social development scales used in the study.

Solomon and Pangle (1966) attempted to assess physical, intellectual, and social changes resulting from the participation of educable retarded boys in a structured physical education program for 45 minutes a day over a period of eight weeks. This study indicated that significant improvement in physical fitness performance resulted from participation in the physical education activities. These gains remained during a six-week post-experiment follow-up period. No changes in mental ability, level of aspiration, or self-concept were observed in this study. Immediate reinforcement, or knowledge of results of participation in physical education activities, was found to produce more improvement than delayed feedback.

SUMMARY

The physical and learning characteristics of mentally retarded children are analyzed in order to point out the needs of these children and to document the effectiveness of certain physical education programs. Handicapped children require instruction in physical fitness, motor skills, and recreational activities; these items are "musts" for inclusion in physical education programs. The research that has been completed indicates that retarded children can improve their physical fitness and motor skill performance. Several studies indicated that some aspects of mental ability may improve from participation in physical activity programs. In all probability, the improvement in mental test scores resulted from increased motivation, or some similar factor, rather than an increase in some innate capacity. This finding, however, has not received extensive investigation.

Sound instructional programs must be based on research for two main reasons: to determine the needs of these children in general, and to determine the individual needs of each child. From these data the physical educator should be able to develop his individualized activity prescription. However, testing must go beyond these limits, and include further evaluation to insure the effectiveness of the prescription. Hopefully the teacher will not stop at this point either. A great service would be performed to educators and students alike if programs are written up and evaluated in terms of effectiveness. We have far to travel; every contribution, regardless of the degree of sophistication, is an important factor.

REFERENCES

Auxter, D. M.: Strength and flexibility of differentially diagnosed educable mentally retarded boys. *Res. Quart.* 37:455–461, 1961.

Beck, S.: Present status of physical education in special classes for the educable mentally handicapped. *Amer. J. Ment. Defic.* 61:117–120, 1956.

Benda, C. E.: *The Child with Mongolism (Congenital Acromicria).* New York: Grune & Statton, 1960.

Brace, David K.: Report of national survey results. *Challenge,* Nov., 1966.

Brace, David K.: Physical education and recreation for mentally retarded pupils in public schools in the United States. *Abstracts of Research Papers.* Washington, D.C.: AAHPER, 1967.

Brown, Joe: Comparative performance of trainable mentally retarded on the Kraus-Weber test. *Res. Quart.* 38:348–354, 1967.

Corder, W. Owens: Effects of physical education on the intellectual, physical and social development of educable mentally retarded boys. (Nashville: George Peabody College for Teachers, Special Education Project, 1965.)

Cratty, Bryant J.: *Developmental Sequences of Perceptual-Motor Tasks: Movement Activities for Neurologically Handicapped and Retarded Children and Youth.* Freeport, L.I., N.Y.: Educational Activities, Inc., 1967.

Culley, W. J., et al.: Heights and weights of mentally retarded children. *Amer. J. Ment. Defic.* 68:203–210, 1963.

Denny, M. R.: Learning and performance, In: H. A. Stevens and R. Heber (Eds.): *Mental Retardation: A Review of Research,* Chicago: University of Chicago Press, 1964.

Drowatzky, John N.: Physical education and the brain-injured child. *J. Assoc. Phys. Ment. Rehab.* 19:124–126, 1965.

Drowatzky, John N.: *Evaluation of a Residential Camp Program for Mentally Retarded Children.* Toledo, Ohio: The University of Toledo, 1967.

Drowatzky, John N.: *Evaluation of a Residential Camp Program for Mentally Retarded Children.* Toledo, Ohio: The University of Toledo, 1968.

Ellis, N. R., Pryer, Margaret W., Distefano, M. K., Jr., and Pryer, R. S.: Learning in mentally defective, normal and superior subjects. *Amer. J. Ment. Defic.* 64:725–734, 1960.

Espenschade, Anna S.: Motor performance in adolescence. *Monogr. Soc. Res. Child Devel.* Vol. 5, No. 1, 1940.

Francis R. J., and Rarick, G. L.: Motor characteristics of the mentally retarded. *Amer. J. Ment. Defic.* 63:292–311, 1959.

Greenfell, James E.: The effect of a structured physical education program on the physical fitness and motor educability of the mentally retarded school children in Whitman County, Washington. (MA thesis, Washington State University, 1965.)

Heebøll-Nielsen, K.: The physical performance of mentally retarded patients and their possibilities for being trained—investigated with psycho-technical tests. *Communications from the Danish National Assoc. for Infantile Paralysis,* Nr. 25, 1967.

Howe, Clifford E.: A comparison of motor skills of mentally retarded and normal children. *Exceptional Child.* 25:353–354, 1959.

Jones, H. E.: *Motor Performance and Growth.* Berkeley: University of California Press, 1949.

Lipman, R. S.: Learning: Verbal, perceptual-motor, and classical conditioning. In: N. R. Ellis (Ed.): *Handbook of Mental Deficiency.* New York: McGraw-Hill, 1963, pp. 391–423.

McCloy, Charles H., and Young, Norma D.: *Tests and Measurements in Health and Physical Education.* New York: Appleton-Century-Crofts, 1954.

Malpass, L. F.: Motor skills in mental deficiency. In: N. R. Ellis (Ed.): *Handbook of Mental Deficiency.* New York: McGraw-Hill, 1963, pp. 602–631.

Meredith, H. V.: The rhythm of physical growth. *Univer. Iowa Stud. Child Welf.* Vol. 11, No. 3, 1935.

Metheny, E.: The present status of strength testing for children of elementary school age. *Res. Quart.* 12:115–130, 1941.

Neilson, N. P., and Cozens, F. W.: *Achievement Scales in Physical Education Activities for Boys and Girls in Elementary and Junior High Schools.* Sacramento, Calif.: Department of Education, 1934.

Oliver, James N.: The effect of physical conditioning exercises and activities on the mental characteristics of educationally subnormal boys. *Brit. J. Educ. Psychol.* 28:155–165, 1958.

Rarick, G. L., et al.: *The Motor Performance and Physical Fitness of Educable Mentally Retarded Children.* Madison: University of Wisconsin, 1967.

Sengstock, Wayne L.: Physical fitness of mentally retarded boys. *Res. Quart.* 37:113–120, 1966.

Shotick, Andrew, and Thate, Charles: Reactions of a group of educable mentally handicapped children to a program of physical education. *Exceptional Child.* 26:248–252, 1960.

Solomon, Amiel, and Pangle, Roy: *The Effects of a Structured Physical Education Program on Physical, Intellectual, and Self-concept Development of Educable Retarded Boys.* Nashville: George Peabody College (Department of Health and Physical Education), 1966.

Stevens, H. A., and Heber, R. (Eds.): *Mental Retardation: A Review of Research.* Chicago: University of Chicago Press, 1964, pp. 91–92.

Woodward, M., and Stern, D. J.: Developmental patterns of severely subnormal children. *Brit. J. Educ. Psychol.* 33:10–12, 1963.

CHAPTER 4

The Learning Process

How do we learn? What does the learning process consist of? These questions have interested men for many years. The first scientifically organized attempts to study learning phenomena began around 1850 with the advent of experimental psychology. Since that time, many scientists have investigated the study of learning, among them educational psychologists and physical educators.

Today we know that much of life, including the necessary survival skills, is dependent upon learning. Motor activities, academic pursuits, attitudes and prejudices, social interaction and communication: all of these can be taught— and learned. Learning, of course, implies change, although more than mere change may be involved. For our purposes, learning will be defined as the modification of behavior which results from training procedures or environmental conditions acting upon the individual. This does not imply that the individual is only a passive receptor, but rather that various environmental changes will cause the person to react and learn. It appears that during this reaction process (which may be either visible or unseen) learning will occur.

Training and environmental conditions are not the only factors contributing to behavioral changes. Growth or maturation may also be an important element in the modification of behavior. If a behavioral alteration develops through a regular sequence, without reference to practice, then maturation, rather than learning, may be the cause of the modification. In other words, if training procedures do not modify or speed up the behavioral changes, then training cannot be considered the primary causal factor and the changes should not be classified as having been learned.

The basis for the acquisition of most skills does not provide a clearcut distinction between learning and maturation, but represents a complex interaction of these and other elements. All people are continually exposed to a variety of conditions which cause behavioral changes. Typical environmental conditions producing learning are observations, social interaction, experimental and manipulative behavior, physical activity, satisfaction of biological needs, and the like.

The basic theories of learning were, for many years, divided into two broad categories—the connectionist theories and the cognitive theories. The various connectionist interpretations of learning, in spite of differences, agree that learning consists of an association, or connection, that is formed between a stimulus and a response or responses. On the other hand, the cognitive theorists were concerned with the various perceptions, beliefs, or attitudes that an individual has about his environment and the manner in which these various "cognitions," or mental activities, determine his behavior. The important aspect of cognitive theories dealt with the manner in which the cognitions were modified by experience.

The stimulus-response (S-R) theorists or connectionists have been concerned with learning and behavior patterns that are mechanistic in nature, with a given input or stimulus yielding a predictable response. Trial and error behavior, characterized by random movement and numerous errors initially with slow and irregular progress toward the goal, is typical of this kind of learning.

In contrast, the cognitive theorists noted that we have choices in our responses and can select behaviors that are appropriate to differing situations. Based on past experiences we learn, not specific responses, but expectancies, ideas, and attitudes that are used to select responses. Most cognitive psychologists studied the learning that occurred suddenly and was accompanied by understanding. Such learning is resistant to forgetting and may be applied to a wide variety of situations. This learning, consisting of an understanding of the logical relationships between the means and the end, is called insight.

At first glance it would appear that these two approaches to the study of learning were not reconcilable. Recently, however, the differences between these two approaches have diminished and today a balanced view of learning requires that both be considered. The relationship between connective and cognitive learning will be utilized in the remainder of this chapter in a description of motor activity and learning, basic learning theories concerning motor learning, and motor learning in mental retardates.

MOTOR ACTIVITY AND LEARNING

We have defined learning as a change in the level of functioning. One has only to reflect on the changes that take place from birth until adulthood to note the magnitude of change. The newborn infant has a repertoire of reflexive acts while the adult has a series of volitional perceptual-motor actions that have developed through a series of assimilations. It should be emphasized that learning at every level, from infancy through adulthood, requires experience. According to Jean Piaget (Flavell, 1963; p. 84), the principles that are learned "become progressively more internalized and schematic by reducing perceptual and motor supports, e.g., moving from object to symbols of objects, from motor action to speech, etc."

The internalization is the process through which the environment acquires meaning. Once meanings have been acquired, the person no longer relies only upon sensation, but rather on conceptions and perceptions that depend on motor activity. The process of developing perceptual-motor skills will serve as the basis from which a discussion of learning principles will follow. Inasmuch as Piaget has probably studied and written more about the developmental patterns of children than any other author, the following brief description of his work will illustrate the relationship of motor activity to other aspects of development.

Piaget's Developmental Psychology

The first period, and perhaps the most important with which Piaget is concerned, is the stage of *sensory-motor development*. This stage of development begins with birth, when it is characterized by reflexes. The reflexes present at birth appear to contain the characteristics of functioning that will persist as constants throughout development. From this rudimentary beginning, the child quickly develops sensory-motor patterns that parallel and assist with the development of visual and auditory meanings. As the sensory-motor stage progresses, the child begins to generalize his motor patterns and coordinate simple individual patterns into new and more complex behaviors. This generalization and formation of new behaviors enable the child to develop important new abilities. For the first time, he is able to make changes in the environment and to learn the relationship of objects to each other and to himself. As this stage ends, the child has learned new means, first through physical experimentation and later through mental combinations. In this way, goal-directed behavior develops from early sensory-motor activities.

While this period persists as a separate entity for only the first 18 months of life, sensory-motor activities continue to exert important influences on development throughout life. Perhaps this is best expressed by Flavell's (1963, p. 121) remarks concluding his discussion of sensory-motor development:

> With the advent of the capacity to represent actions rather than simply to perform them, the sensory-motor period draws to a close and the child is ready for an analogous but even more extended and tortuous apprenticeship in the use of symbols. The end of the sensory-motor period is thus synchronous with the beginning of the preoperational period. This does not, of course, mean that the child no longer continues to develop in the sensory-motor sphere. But it does mean that henceforth the most advanced *intellectual* adaptations of which a given child is capable will take place in a conceptual-symbolic rather than purely sensory-motor arena.

Piaget was concerned not only with the emergence and consolidation of sensory-motor patterns, but also with six special developments that arise from the child's initial reflexive adaptation patterns. These developments include the ability to imitate and play, the understanding of the characteristics of objects, and the development of the concepts of space, time, and causality. Each of these capacities—imitation, play, object concept, space, time, and causality—is important in the child's future growth and development. For Piaget, sensory-motor abilities have a very special and useful role.

After the sensory-motor stage, the child progresses through three additional aspects of development. The *preoperational* stage (1 1/2 to 7 years of age) is characterized by a child who is conscious of his existence in a world of permanent objects that are separate from him and have causal effects on each other. However, his behavior is directly linked to what he perceives and does at any given moment. In the next stage, *concrete operations* (7 to 11 years), the child's thinking is no longer restricted to the presence of physical objects, but he is unable to make adequate inferences from verbal information alone; it must be combined with movement or other types of information. Finally, in the *abstract operations* stage (11 years and older) the child achieves adult abilities and characteristics. "Hence Piaget's theory permits him to see adult logical operations as sensory-motor actions which have undergone a succession of transformations, rather than a different species of behavior entirely" (Flavell, 1963; p. 83).

It is important to note the primacy placed on motor activities by Piaget. In his scheme of child development, sensory-motor intelligence provides the foundation for later intellectual development; it is sensory-motor ability from which and in which perception develops and evolves (Flavell, 1963). Piaget's work may be extended beyond the realm of the normal child. For example, Woodward (1963) has suggested that this theory be applied to the study of such problems as cognitive functions, measurement of developmental levels, and performance on learning tasks in mental retardates. Future research will indicate the applicability of Piaget's procedures to mental retardation.

Kephart's Perceptual-Motor Bases

The perceptual-motor aspects of learning were originally studied by N. C. Kephart to develop a rationale for dealing with the child with learning disabilities. As most of our classroom experiences are symbolic (verbal or written), Kephart (1964) believed that all such presentations are based on the fundamental assumption "that the child has established an adequate orientation to the basic realities of the universe—space and time" (p. 201). Kephart studied the establishment of this orientation to space and time extensively.

The perceptual-motor aspects of learning are based on the knowledge that the child's first interactions with his environment are motor and his first learnings are motor learnings. Inasmuch as we can learn both motor skills and motor patterns, Kephart (1964) distinguishes between the two. He defined a motor skill as a specific specialized motor act that is performed with a high degree of precision. The motor pattern, on the other hand, requires lesser degrees of precision, but broader degrees of variability. A motor skill is designed for a specific result and only limited variation is possible, while a motor pattern has a much broader purpose and allows extensive variation.

This wide applicability of motor patterns makes them an essential part of information-gathering during the child's basic stages of development. According to Kephart (1964) and Godfrey and Kephart (1969), four motor patterns appear to be of particular significance:

1. *Balance and Maintenance of Posture.* The essential contribution of this motor pattern is that the child acquires knowledge of the nature of the force of gravity and his relationship to it. An extension of this knowledge results in the development of spatial relationships (up-down, left-right, front-back). Inasmuch as subsequent exploratory activities will involve movement, posture and balance become important contributing factors to the more active types of exploration.

2. *Locomotion.* The locomotor skills move the child through space and enable him to investigate the relationships within the space around him. Movement through space enables the child to learn about the position of objects in space and their relationship to each other.

3. *Contact.* The contact skills of reach, grasp, and release enable the child to manipulate objects and learn about relationships within objects (i.e., shape, form, and size constancy).

4. *Receipt and Propulsion.* These skills allow the child to investigate movements in space. Receipt skills enable the child to make contact with moving objects and he imparts movement to objects through propulsion.

The skills and characteristics used to support future learning develop from these motor patterns. Included among these are gross motor skills, eye-hand coordination, laterality, directionality, ability to stop, dexterity, temporal-spatial translation, form perception, and body image (Kephart, 1960).

The child must learn about time as well as space. Kephart (1964) feels that motor activities teach the temporal relationships of synchrony (point of temporal origin), rhythm (stable, equal time intervals), and sequencing (ordering events in time). This motor-temporal system is projected onto environmental events just as the motor-spatial is used in the perception of outside objects.

Although this theory was not developed specifically for programs with mentally retarded children, it indicates the importance that Kephart attaches to the development of adequate motor abilities. Because of the fundamental importance of motor patterns, the role of motor development in providing adequate movement and adaptive behavior in retarded children cannot be overlooked.

PRINCIPLES OF LEARNING

In the earlier parts of this chapter, learning was defined as a change in the level of functioning at which a person operates. The close relationship between motor activity and the learning of perceptions and concepts has been emphasized. However, little or no mention was made of how we learn. This section will present different principles of learning that have been derived from research conducted in the past. As principles are considered it is important to remember that learning has three important elements: (1) it is a change in behavior, for better or worse; (2) this change occurs as a result of practice or experience; and, (3) the change is relatively permanent. Learning consists of many phenomena which often occur under rather complicated conditions. Only those phenomena that are most common and most appropriate to the instruction of mentally retarded children will be considered here.

Association

One characteristic of most learning situations is that some association or connection, either in time or place, occurs between two events. The nature of this association in the central nervous system is not understood, but it apparently forms the basis for abstract abilities and may be defined as the mechanism in the brain that enables one process in the brain to become connected, or associated, with another. Further, once this association has been formed, the initiation of one process will trigger the second process. These processes may be either representations of environmental stimuli (sensations) or motor actions. Thus, there may be sensory associations in which two or more sensations are associated and stimulus-response associations in which connections are formed between a stimulus and responses. Because the formation between a stimulus (S) and a response (R) is most easily studied, the next few paragraphs will discuss the formation of associations using stimulus-response examples which are known as classical conditioning, instrumental conditioning, and insightful learning.

Classical Conditioning. As early as the 1880's, Ivan Pavlov, a Russian physiologist, provided psychology with one of its most useful tools, an understanding of the process of classical conditioning. All animals, humans not excepted, are born with certain S-R connections that we call reflexes, or in the case of complex patterns of reflexes, tropisms. Through conditioning, the organism is able to develop a multitude of new S-R associations. The great value of conditioning is that it provides the means for each response in the original repertoire of reflexes to be elicited by a large variety of new stimuli in addition to the stimulus that originally induced it.

The basic conditioning experiment was discovered by chance during Pavlov's study of salivation and gastric secretions. When meat powder was placed in a dog's mouth, saliva flowed in response. Pavlov observed that if he regularly provided a unique stimulus, such as the sound of a bell, just before the animal was given food, eventually the sound of the bell alone would elicit the response which was originally brought forth by the food. Pavlov's procedure in animal experimentation consisted of ringing a bell and almost immediately following the bell tone with food. The bell and meat powder would be presented in this manner for a number of trials. Finally, the sound of the bell, without presentation of food, caused the dog to salivate. Typical results from this type of experiment are presented in Figure 4—1.

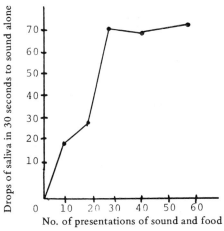

Figure 4—1. Development of a conditioned salivary response in one dog. (Modified from Mednik, 1964.)

The stimulus (meat power) which originally elicited a reflex response (salivation) was termed the *unconditioned stimulus* (UCS) and the reflex response was called the *unconditioned response* (UCR). In our example, the sound of the bell, which served as a signal for the food, is named the *conditioned stimulus* (CS) and once the response (salivation) becomes paired with the GS, it is then called a *conditioned response* (CR). This is presented diagrammatically in Figure 4—2.

Further experiments have indicated that environmental events have even greater effects on behavior than was indicated by simple classical conditioning experiments. For example, a response elicited by one stimulus through classical conditioning can be "transferred" to a new stimulus. This "higher-order" conditioning process is important in our understanding of human learning. Classical conditioning does not have a large role in our educational process, but it does illustrate how sensory-motor patterns, imitation, play, and the like are able to develop from the infant's birth reflexes.

Instrumental Conditioning. The second basic type of conditioning, less well-known outside the field of psychology, is called instrumental condition-

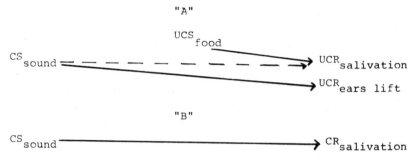

Figure 4–2. "A" represents the pairing of the unconditioned stimulus with the stimulus to be conditioned. "B" represents the completion of the conditioning process when the conditioned stimulus alone will elicit the conditioned response. (Modified from Staats and Staats, 1964.)

ing. The typical laboratory demonstration would consist of a hungry rat placed into a small box with a small bar mounted inside which the rat can push. Whenever the animal presses the bar, a small pellet of food is dropped into a tray for the animal to eat. Through trial and error practice, the response of bar pressing becomes more and more prevalent. It, therefore, becomes one of the most prominent aspects of the rat's behavior as long as the rat remains hungry and continues to receive food when it depresses the bar. Typical records obtained in this type of experiment are shown in Figure 4–3.

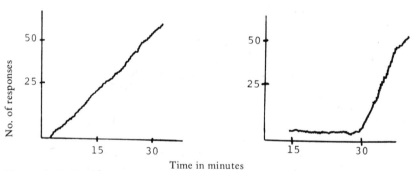

Figure 4–3. Typical response curves obtained from a bar-pressing experiment with rats. (Modified from Kimble, 1961.)

Perhaps the psychologist most concerned with such types of conditioning over the past few years has been B. F. Skinner (1938, 1953), who referred to classical conditioning as "respondent" conditioning to emphasize that it was largely reflexive in nature since the organism simply responds to the stimulus. Instrumental conditioning was called "operant" conditioning because the individual is able to "operate" upon his environment (which includes his own body) to either produce some stimulus event or cause a change in some event. Operant behavior involves trial and error learning and the response to the behavioral sequence must be rewarded in some manner. Examples of operant behavior include such actions as shooting a basketball at the hoop, which produces the reward of a goal; turning on the television set with the resulting reward of sound and picture; or lifting weights which may result in physical changes, a feeling of accomplishment, or perhaps social acceptance. Thus, this broad class of responses involves, for the most part, the use of skeletal muscles and voluntary responses (Bijou and Baer, 1961).

Learning is much broader than the processes studied in classical and instrumental conditioning experiments. However, many scientists have studied conditioning as a prototypical form of learning and it is important to understand the process involved in order to evaluate their work. There are both advantages and disadvantages to the use of conditioning to explain learning. The chief advantage is its simplicity and predictability; the main weakness is its inability to account for all learning situations. As we shall see, insightful learning supplements these traditional types of learning in an explanation of behavior.

Insightful Learning. It is now generally recognized that learning involves more than the gradual acquisition of new behaviors through trial and error experiences. Learning is often discontinuous, error curves show sharp drops without warning, and the kind of error that is made in one trial may not be present in the next (Hebb, 1949). Learning may occur suddenly and be accompanied by a feeling of understanding. Such learning is resistant to forgetting and may be applied to a wide variety of situations. Insightful learning, which consists of an understanding of the logical relationships between the means and the end, is based upon previously acquired conceptions and perceptions. The better these precepts and concepts are established, the more quickly learning will occur.

Tolman (1942) postulated two situations that are basic to insightful learning. The first, *sign-Gestalt-expectations*, holds that an individual has expectations that the world is organized in certain ways and that certain things lead to others. *Place learning*, the second situation, emphasizes that the learner does not move from a starting point to his goal through a fixed sequence of movements, but is capable of behavior that varies appropriately to changed conditions. Experience is thus an important factor in insight for without appropriate experiences, insightful learning will not occur.

Most of us, if our developmental level is sufficiently high, use classical, instrumental, and insightful learning during our lives. Perhaps Hebb (1949) best expresses the manner in which these types of learning interrelate. He described two stages of learning, *primary* and *later* learning. Primary learning begins at birth and predominates until about 12 years of age. During this period, environmental control is established over behavior as sensory events continually impose a new type of organization over the cortex through classical and instrumental conditioning. Later learning is more conceptual in nature, involving patterns and events whose parts, at least, are familiar and already have a number of associations. Prompt learning is possible when the stimulus triggers well-organized concepts; otherwise, more trials are required for learning. Characteristic adult learning takes place in a few trials, or as single-trial insightful learning in contrast to the repetitive, trial and error nature of primary learning.

Reinforcement

The first reinforcement psychologist was E. L. Thorndike (1913), who presented the law of effect. This law referred to the fact that a stimulus-response connection may be either strengthened or weakened as a result of its consequences. In other words, if a stimulus was followed by a response which was in turn followed by a "satisfier," the stimulus-response bond would become strengthened. Conversely, if the stimulus was followed by a response and then by an "annoyer," the connection would become weakened. This law was modified until it became the familiar statement that satisfying consequences will reinforce stimulus-response bonds.

It remained for Skinner (1938, 1953) to elaborate on the effect of reinforcement on learning. He studied both positive and negative reinforcers in terms of their effect upon behavior. From this work, he observed that instrumental (operant or voluntary) behavior may have four kinds of consequences. It may: (1) produce positive reinforcers, (2) remove or avoid negative reinforcers, (3) produce negative reinforcers, or (4) remove or avoid positive reinforcers. If the behavior either produces positive reinforcers or removes negative reinforcers (i.e., eliminate fatigue or pain), it will be strengthened and consequently repeated. On the other hand, if negative reinforcers (fatigue or pain) are produced or if positive reinforcers are removed, then the responses will not be repeated and the behavior is extinguished. Additional concepts about the nature of reinforcement were set forth in his discussions of shaping and schedules of reinforcement.

Schedules of Reinforcement. The work of Ferster and Skinner (1957) indicated that regardless of whether a response is reinforced each time it occurs or whether it is reinforced only intermittently, the behavior will be acquired. When the response is reinforced on an intermittent basis, the procedure is considered to be a schedule of reinforcement. Two broad classes of schedules, a ratio schedule and an interval schedule, have been developed through laboratory study. In general, it has been observed that when reinforcement schedules are followed, a faster rate of responding is achieved and the behavior is more difficult to extinguish. A practical example of this may be observed by watching people manipulate the slot machine in Las Vegas. The schedules of reinforcement used in the study of learning are summarized in Table 4—1.

Table 4—1. Summary of Schedules of Reinforcement Used to Promote Instrumental Conditioning

I. *Ratio Schedule:*	A fixed number of responses must occur before a reinforcement is obtained.
1. *Fixed ratio.*	The ratio of reinforced to unreinforced responses does not change (i.e., every third response is reinforced).
2. *Variable ratio.*	The ratio of reinforced to unreinforced responses changes after each reinforcement (i.e., first after one response, then 3, then 7 responses, etc.). There is no regular pattern of reinforcement.
II. *Interval Schedule:*	The amount of elapsed time will determine when reinforcement is given. Reinforcement is independent of the number of responses made.
1. *Fixed interval.*	The reinforcement is given for the first response made after the lapse of a specified time period and this procedure is followed after each lapse of the predetermined time period (i.e., after every three minutes).
2. *Variable interval.*	The reinforcement is offered at different time intervals (i.e., after 1 minute, 2 minutes, 5 minutes, 3 minutes, etc.) and no regular pattern is followed.

From Ferster and Skinner, 1957.

Shaping. Shaping of behavior is the process of rewarding responses that approximate the desired response. Usually, the initial rewards are made to rather gross approximations, but slowly and regularly the rewards are given only to those responses that more closely resemble the final desired response. Many different reinforcers, such as praise or candy, have been used to shape behavior of children. Perhaps the following practical example of shaping behavior in a seriously disturbed child will illustrate this technique:

> In addition to numerous other difficulties, this boy was practically blind after a series of operations for cataracts when he was two years old. It was extremely important for him to wear glasses, and this behavior was shaped by successive approximations to the desired final response of continuously wearing the glasses. The child was placed in a room where several empty glasses frames were lying around. Whenever he picked up one of these, he was reinforced with small pieces of candy or fruit. Soon he touched the frames quite often, but it was extremely difficult to shape the next step in the chain, putting the glasses on in the proper way. The therapists then arranged to use more powerful reinforcers by making the bites of lunch contingent upon having the glasses closer and closer to the proper wearing position. In a very short time, with this more powerful reinforcer, it was possible to shape both the behavior of putting on the glasses and the behavior of looking through them after they had been put on properly. The boy was soon wearing his glasses for 12 hours each day. (Morgan and King, 1966, p. 91.)

Motivation

It is well known that our performance varies from time to time. One of the factors responsible for this variation in performance is motivation. Motivation has such a pronounced influence on performance that it has been called the "energizer of behavior." There are two broad categories of need or drives that motivate behavior. They are called the primary and secondary drives. The primary drives are physiological in nature (i.e., rest, thirst, hunger) and appear to be unlearned. Secondary drives, in contrast, are believed to be learned. They are psychological or social influences such as the need for achievement, security, power, prestige, recognition, and the like. Both primary and secondary drives are equally important in controlling behavior and interact in many situations.

Motivation has a mixed effect upon learning and motor performance. Situations that are either not motivating or overly motivating can disrupt learning and performance. There is an optimal range of motivating conditions essential for most efficient learning and performance. Unfortunately, no reliable test exists to enable the teacher to judge when optimal conditions exist. The teacher must rely upon his own judgment and experience in order to develop optimal conditions.

In spite of the fact that no objective test exists for measuring the motivation of children, certain basic factors may be taken into account when attempting to improve learning or performance. The most basic fact is that the child has learned certain schemes of behavior that are satisfying. Each child acquires a set of basic needs, many of which are acquired in cultural context. The further development of these needs depends upon the child's state of development, the younger the child, the more limited the needs. The teacher may consider the following to motivate a child toward a better performance: the need for autonomy, the need for social acceptance, the need for recognition, the desire for support from others, and the like. The task of the teacher becomes one of observing the child, determining which motives are important to the child, and then using the information in a constructive manner to improve the learning situation.

Distribution of Practice

One important aspect of training that has been used to produce behavioral change is the amount of time allotted for practice sessions. The general consensus of research indicates that during practice trials distributed practice produces a better performance than massed practice. Distributed or spaced practice refers to the condition under which the practice sessions are interspersed with rest periods. It is important to realize that the temporary superiority of distributed practice over massed practice is a factor of performance, rather than learning. If a rest period is allowed after a massed practice session, the individual's performance after rest will not differ from that achieved by distributed practice.

These findings were explained by Hull (1943). He suggested that the superiority of distributed practice results from the existence of an inhibitory state that evokes a need for rest and tends to dissipate spontaneously with rest.

The inhibitory condition that occurs during motor learning is often believed to develop from lack of motivation, boredom, and physical fatigue. The question concerning the relative superiority of these two practice conditions thus becomes one of efficiency. Under conditions where the efficiency of performance during learning is not critical it may be more economical to use massed practice.

Whole or Part Learning

Many researchers have attempted to evaluate the relative merits of presenting material as a unified whole or dividing it into smaller parts for instruction. Generally, research has indicated that the part method is more advantageous when the part forms a unit that is easily separable from a whole, when the whole unit is too large to be understood, or when the motivational value of immediate knowledge of results is desired. The teacher must remember that he has to make provisions to link all the parts together into the whole after they have been fully learned. On the other hand, the whole method appears to be indicated for use when the student has enough intelligence and experience to learn the material quickly, when the practice on the whole can be spaced, and when the material to be learned is meaningful to the student. In actual practice a combination of these two methods, rather than only one or the other, seems to provide the best results. Under this approach, the student starts the practice period with the whole method, and when difficult parts are encountered the part method is used. Finally, the whole method is to unify the instruction. Regardless of whether the teacher uses the whole or part method of instruction, all material to be presented must be meaningful to the student.

Transfer

Nearly everyone has observed that people can transfer what they have learned from one situation to another. According to McGeoch and Irion (1952, p. 346):

> After small amounts of learning early in the life of the individual, every instance of learning is a function of the already learned organization of the subject; that is, all learning is influenced by transfer . . .

Positive transfer is said to occur when a previously learned skill benefits learning or performance in a new situation and, conversely, negative transfer occurs when a previously learned skill hinders learning or performance in a new situation. In a recent publication, Irion (1969) reported that positive transfer is much more likely to occur in skills situations than is negative transfer. In fact, even when optimum conditions of interference are arranged, the negative transfer effects appear to be weak and transitory. Thus, as the child grows and develops we see the learning of a new skill less and less frequently. Rather we observe the putting together of practiced sequences into some new motor skill pattern.

MOTOR SKILL LEARNING IN THE RETARDED

A summary of general learning principles has been presented in this chapter. However, the question remains, "Do retarded children learn motor skills in the same manner as normal children?" While the normal child learns many of his motor skills through incidental means, it appears that the more severely retarded children are unable to accomplish this. These children must receive direct training in the skills they are to acquire.

One technique that is particularly useful in teaching the retarded new motor skills is the shaping of behavior described earlier in this chapter. Recall that the behavior is gradually modified through a series of successive approximations until the desired skill is obtained. Through this training, the teacher strives to bring motor actions under the control of external verbal stimulation. Because the severely retarded child may not learn well through imitation, often a three step progression is followed during the training program. These steps are outlined as follows:

First step: demonstrate and provide assistance through manipulation of the body part(s) while giving verbal cues (i.e., "lift the block").

Second step: demonstrate (without assistance) and give verbal cues.

Third step: provide verbal cue without any demonstration.

According to Linford (1968) higher levels of motor skill development may be obtained by bringing the natural play skills of the child under the control of the teacher's verbal stimuli and by following a behavioral modification program such as described above for absent skills.

Evans (1968), Lipman (1963), and Zeaman and House (1963) have indicated the importance of short, accurate, and concise directions to retardates. If maximum value of instruction is to be obtained, the teacher must be careful not to present many confusing stimuli and difficult concepts at one time. Inasmuch as the retardate has difficulty locating the pertinent characteristics of a stimulus and is easily distracted, the extraneous characteristics of the environment should be removed whenever possible. Furthermore, learning may be facilitated if the important characteristics of a stimulus (or situation) are highlighted or emphasized in some manner.

Performance is substantially related to intelligence and age in retarded children (Ellis, *et al.,* 1960; Evans, 1968), and rate of learning is dependent upon the nature of the learning task, the intellectual level of the student, and his related handicaps (Barnett, *et al.,* 1960). The teacher must realize that although performance levels and rates of learning may differ, all children require considerable experience in both specific problem situations and problem situations of a more general nature. In the more severely retarded, learning will be basically of a trial and error nature; very little in the nature of insightful learning that requires concepts will be possible.

Several studies have indicated that various practice conditions have differing effects upon normal and retarded persons. Ellis, Pryer, and Barnett (1960) observed the performance of normal and mildly retarded subjects practicing under massed and distributed conditions. After comparing both the initial acquisition and retention of the skills, the investigators reported that the normal subjects performed at a significantly higher level on all phases of the experiment and retained relatively more over the retention trials. In a second study, normal and educable retarded subjects practiced to achieve a common standard defined by Wright and Hearn (1964); following a rest period they were given 10 additional trials. Analysis of this data showed the normal subjects exhibiting more reminiscence than the retardates. These two studies suggest that mildly retarded individuals may suffer less performance decrement from mass practice than normal children.

A recent study conducted by Baumeister and others (1966) reported findings that differed from the two previous studies. These investigators observed that the initial superiority of normal subjects over retarded subjects diminished with practice. Furthermore, they were unable to observe a more rapid build-up of performance decrement in normals. Comparable amounts of reminiscence were also shown by normals and retardates in this study. The inferiority of the retardates during the initial stages of the task was attributed to inappropriate postural and attentive adjustments while the relatively sharp rate of improvement appeared to result from the rapid development of secondary responses relating to the "set" to respond.

Drowatzky (1970) has reported that trainable retarded subjects may not respond to practice conditions in the same manner as the less severely retarded persons. His results suggest that trainable mentally retarded persons may be penalized by massed practice during the initial stages of learning. Large numbers of retarded subjects participating in his study were unable to learn a tracking task under massed practice. This failure appeared to be caused by their continued inability to make appropriate postural and attentive adjustments coupled with the inability to develop the proper response set. Apparently a distributed schedule of practice allowed the retardates to overcome these problems.

The differences in learning curves of educable and trainable retardates are indicated in Figure 4—4. Note that the educable retardates' curve approximates the normal pattern, while little change is evidenced in the trainables' performance.

SUMMARY

Although there are several different theories of learning, most investigators agree that motor skills and motor activity are essential for any degree of

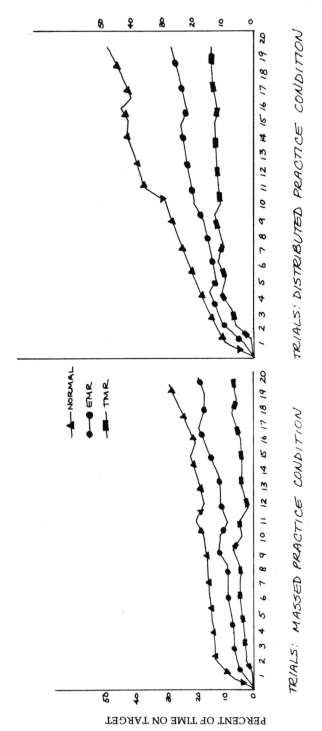

Figure 4–4. Comparison of massed and distributed practice learning curves obtained for educable retarded, trainable retarded, and normal subjects. [Data obtained from Ellis, Pryer, and Barnett (1960) and Drowatzky (1970).].

educational achievement. For the retarded, motor skills form the basis for self-help and safety activities, assist in the development of a favorable self-image, and help the child achieve some level of recreational and occupational independence. Motor skills must be taught to the retarded child in easily understood units that are later integrated into a meaningful perception.

REFERENCES

Barnett, C. D., *et al.*: Learning in familial and brain-injured defectives. *Amer. J. Ment. Defic.* 64:894–901, 1960.

Baumeister, A. A., Hawkins, W. F., and Holland, J.: Motor learning and knowledge of results. *Amer. J. Ment. Defic.* 70:590–594, 1966.

Bijou, S. W., and Baer, D. M.: *Child Development: Volume I: A Systematic and Empirical Theory.* New York: Appleton-Century-Crofts, 1961.

Drowatzky, John N.: Effects of massed and distributed practice schedules upon the acquisition of pursuit rotor tracking by normal and mentally retarded subjects. *Res. Quart.* 41:32–38, 1970.

Ellis, N. R., Pryer, M. W., and Barnett, C. D.: Motor learning and retention in normals and defectives. *Percept. Motor Skills* 10:83–91, 1960.

Ellis, N. R., *et al.*: Learning in mentally defective, normal and superior subjects. *Amer. J. Ment. Defic.* 64:725–734, 1960.

Evans, R. A.: Some stimulus factors involved in the discrimination learning of mental retardates. *Amer. J. Ment. Defic.* 73:61–69, 1968.

Ferster, C. B., and Skinner, B. F.: *Schedules of Reinforcement.* New York: Appleton-Century-Crofts, 1957.

Flavell, J. H.: *The Developmental Psychology of Jean Piaget.* Princeton, N. J.: D. Van Nostrand Company, 1963.

Godfrey, B. B., and Kephart, N. C.: *Movement Patterns and Motor Education.* New York: Appleton-Century-Crofts, 1969.

Hebb, D. O.: *Organization of Behavior.* New York: John Wiley & Sons, 1949.

Hull, C. L.: *Principles of Behavior.* New York: Appleton-Century-Crofts, 1943.

Irion, A. L.: Historical Introduction, In: E. A. Bilodeau and I. Mc. Bilodeau (Eds.): *Principles of Skill Acquisition.* New York: Academic Press, 1969, pp. 1–31.

Jones, W. R., and Ellis, N. R.: Inhibitory potential in rotary pursuit acquisition by normal and defective subjects. *J. Exp. Psychol.* 63:534–537, 1962.

Kephart, N. C.: *The Slow Learner in the Classroom.* Columbus, Ohio: Charles E. Merrill, 1960.

Kephart, N. C.: Perceptual-motor aspects of learning disabilities. *Exceptional Child.* 31:201–206, 1964.

Kimble, G. A.: *Hilgard and Marquis' Conditioning and Learning,* 2nd ed. New York: Appleton-Century-Crofts, 1961.

Linford, A. G. The operant pairing of external verbal stimuli and motor responses as an aid to the physical and self-care development of severely retarded children. (Unpublished manuscript, University of Illinois, 1968.)

Lipman, R. S.: Learning: Verbal, perceptual-motor and classical conditioning. In: N. R. Ellis (Ed.): *Handbook of Mental Deficiency.* New York: McGraw-Hill, 1963.

McGeoch, J. A., and Irion, A. L.: *The Psychology of Human Learning,* 2nd ed. New York: Longmans, Green and Co., 1952.

Mednick, S. A.: *Learning.* Englewood Cliffs, N. J.: Prentice-Hall, 1964.

Morgan, C. T., and King, R. A.: *Introduction to Psychology,* 3rd ed. New York: McGraw-Hill, 1966.

Skinner, B. F.: *The Behavior of Organisms.* New York: Appleton-Century-Crofts, 1938.

Skinner, B. F.: *Science and Human Behavior.* New York: Macmillan, 1953.

Staats, A. W., and Staats, C. K.: *Complex Human Behavior: A Systematic Extension of Learning Principles.* New York: Holt, Rinehart and Winston, 1964.

Thorndike, E. L.: *The Psychology of Learning.* New York: Teacher's College, 1913.

Tolman, E. C.: *Purposive Behavior in Animals and Men.* New York: Appleton-Century-Crofts, 1942.

Woodward, M.: The application of Piaget's theory to research in mental deficiency. In: N. R. Ellis (Ed.): *Handbook of Mental Deficiency.* New York: McGraw-Hill, 1963.

Wright, Logan, and Hearn, Curry B., Jr.: Reactive inhibition in normals and defectives as measured from a common performance criterion. *J. Gen. Psychol.* 71:57–64, 1964.

Zeaman, D., and House, B. J.: The role of attention in retardate discrimination learning. In: N. R. Ellis (Ed.): *Handbook of Mental Deficiency.* New York: McGraw-Hill, 1963.

CHAPTER **5**

Program Development

The increase in the number of special classes and services for mentally retarded children represents progress and reflects the educational philosophy that each child is entitled to an education appropriate to his abilities and needs. However, it still remains for the results of the new programs to demonstrate that they actually serve the purposes for which they are intended. New programs must be carefully planned to avoid perpetuating the weaknesses and mistakes that may have been present in the existing ones that served as models. Our rapidly changing society, which reflects population shifts, changes in the nature of employment opportunities, more leisure time, and increased technological requirements, makes it difficult to develop programs with any degree of permanence.

These factors place the responsibility for program development upon local agencies and teachers. Programs for the retarded must achieve some measure of success in academic training, physical education, and occupational training, and must then be followed by vigorous efforts to integrate the retarded person into the social and occupational opportunities of the community. Communication among teachers and administrators is therefore essential to the success of programs for mentally retarded in order to insure that all instruction and experiences are integrated into a meaningful program.

OBJECTIVES OF PHYSICAL EDUCATION

Goals that were established by the Educational Policies Commission of the *National Education Association* generally form the basis for planning educational programs for the retarded. These goals are: (a) achievement of self-realization, (b) development of proper human relationships, (c) attainment of economic efficiency, (d) development of civic responsibility. In general, these policies must be adapted to the specific needs and abilities of the retarded.

47

Physical education furthers the general goals of education and reflects the particular contributions that may be made to the individual's development through participation in physical activities. Physical education contributes specifically to the individual's development in areas of perceptual-motor skill development, physical fitness, social and emotional development, and leisure time activities. Inasmuch as instruction for retarded children is often necessarily corrective or adaptive in nature, their physical education programs may often include a remedial aspect.

Perceptual-Motor Skills

Because these skills are basic to physical education activities, the main emphasis early in the program should be on the development of the basic movement skills such as running, jumping, throwing, catching, climbing, and the like. Closely allied with these are the various perceptual-motor skills comprising spatial relations, coordination, temporal relations, and the learning of other general perceptions. Once these elementary skills have been mastered, they may be combined and extended into more advanced levels such as striking a ball with a bat, running and kicking a ball, running and catching a ball, and moving about while hopping on one foot. Without a strong emphasis on the fundamentals and improvement in the skill level, however, there will be no advancement for the retarded child in the physical education program.

Physical Fitness

Many retarded children have such low levels of strength and endurance that it is necessary to develop their physical fitness before they are able to participate successfully in the program of skill instruction. They may also require instruction in such commands as "down, up." A pleasant, structured atmosphere will aid the instructor in the establishment of effective student-teacher relationships.

Social Development

Social skills enable the youngster to get along with people and function effectively in group situations. Play and sports activities can be structured to teach the retarded child to play with others, to follow directions, to obey rules, and to accept decisions made by others. Play may also increase self-discipline and self-direction abilities as the retarded child develops security and self-confidence through successful experiences. The camaraderie that develop through interaction with one's peers is an important contribution to social development.

Emotional Development

Happiness is a by-product of effective emotional development. The retarded child must learn to respond to daily failures and frustrations in emotionally sound and socially acceptable ways. Development of basic motor skills and responsibility in the retarded child will increase his opportunities for satisfaction. As improved motor skills increase the retardate's possibilities for participation in work and play activities, the concomitant increase in independence, confidence, recognition, and satisfaction will lead to improved emotional functioning.

Leisure Time Activities

There is a definite need to teach wholesome leisure time activities to retarded children. Instruction in games and other recreational activities may emphasize group participation, as in Drop-the-Handkerchief, Hide and Seek, and Statues; or may require only two or three participants, as in Flies and Grounders or Horse. The important consideration when selecting such activities is to provide each child with the opportunity for success as well as failure. Other recreational activities that are highly beneficial for these children include riding a bicycle or tricycle, swinging, climbing a jungle gym, and climbing trees.

Sports Skill Instruction

Sports instruction may be included in the program after the skill level has been developed to the point where the students are able to participate in the activity. Sports participation is particularly valuable to the development of the less severely retarded children. Besides improving physical fitness and basic skills, participation in sports activities under proper direction can aid greatly in the development of such desirable qualities as sociability, sportsmanship, initiative, and self-confidence. The retarded child has few, if any, other opportunities to interact in a give and take situation.

ESSENTIALS IN PROGRAM DEVELOPMENT

There are two principles which are basic to a physical education program for the handicapped child. First, experiences which lead to concepts must be emphasized. That is, each skill must contribute to the child's understanding of his body, space, or objects; each skill must be reduced to its smallest component, taught piece by piece and reconstructed into the total skill. The child must then be taught how to combine the small units of instruction into a meaningful total. Second, the experiences must be well-organized and integrated. The program should consist of a continual, gradual change as each new activity is presented to the students. This method contrasts with the usual teaching technique in which the whole activity is presented first and then broken into parts for instruction when students experience difficulty in learning.

Normal children learn many motor skills spontaneously by observing other children at play. Retardates appear to have only limited ability in learning motor skills through these incidental means. Moreover, the retardate's functional level is considerably different from either his chronological or mental age. The activities selected for use in his physical education program must be appropriate for the level at which the retardate functions. The following outline illustrates the way in which activities may be used to achieve program objectives. The wide variety of activities that may be used to attain certain objectives allows the instructor to adapt the program to many different functional levels.

I. *Perceptual-Motor Skill Development*
  A. Balance and maintenance of posture
    1. Static balance stunts
    2. Dynamic balance stunts
    3. Balance beam activities
    4. Tumbling and gymnastic activities
    5. Games involving balance
    6. Obstacle course
  B. Locomotion
    1. Basic movement skills
    2. Tag games
    3. Relays
    4. Stunts
    5. Rhythms
    6. Games involving movement
    7. Obstacle course
  C. Contact skills
    1. Activities requiring grasping and manipulation of objects
    2. Chalkboard activities
    3. Block building
    4. Clay modeling
    5. Stringing beads
    6. Marbles
  D. Receipt and propulsion
    1. Throwing and catching
    2. Kicking and trapping
    3. Striking activities
    4. Games involving the above skills
    5. Volleyball
    6. Basketball
    7. Soccer
    8. Football
    9. Softball
II. *Physical Fitness*
  A. Calisthenics
  B. Progressive resistance exercises
  C. Combatives
  D. Stunts and self-testing activities
  E. Vigorous games and relays
  F. Running and tag games
  G. Swimming
  H. Bicycling
  I. Obstacle course

III. *Social Development*
- A. Rhythms
- B. Low organized games and lead-up activities
- C. Sports skills
- D. Relays
- E. Stunts and dual activities

IV. *Leisure Time Activities*
- A. Low organized games and lead-up activities
- B. Sports skills
- C. Playground activities
- D. Aquatics
- E. Bicycling
- F. Individual and dual sports and activities

GUIDELINES IN SELECTING ACTIVITIES

Many of the activities specified for retarded children are basically the same as those of any well-planned physical education program. However, because of the retardate's special characteristics, the activities sometimes require modification and teaching methods must be adjusted to present instruction at a more basic level. The following guidelines are offered as an aid to the teacher in planning a program:

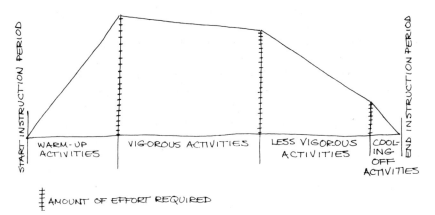

Figure 5–1. Distribution of effort required of students during the physical education period. Note that activities requiring more effort are placed in the middle of the instructional period with provisions for the students to warm-up at the beginning and taper-off at the end of the period.

1. Skills should be selected on the basis of the child's developmental level and needs. The effectiveness of any instruction depends on how well it relates to the child's physical, mental, social, and emotional characteristics.

2. As with any group of children, individual differences must play a role

in the selection of activities. When a class has students with widely varying abilities, the activities selected must make provisions for these differences.

3. Teacher expectancy will greatly influence the child's performance. It is important not to underestimate the children's abilities. The usual tendency is for teachers to set goals for retarded children that are far too easy and the children subsequently fail to reach their potential.

4. The class environment must be carefully structured so that the child participates in a program that provides challenges, success, and freedom from danger. Because of the short attention span and the tendency to be distracted easily, all unnecessary equipment should be kept out of sight except when it is needed. Other distractions must also be kept to a minimum.

5. Whereas the normal child "learns" to play, the more severely retarded child must be "taught" to play. Demonstrations, strong visual and audio cues, and physically guiding a body part through the desired movement are effective teaching techniques.

6. Periodically inspect the instructional area and equipment for hazards, defect, and breakage. The instructor must make every possible provision for the retarded children to participate in safety.

7. The program must be continuously evaluated. Evaluation will enable the instructor to determine whether his educational goals are being attained and provide the basis for making desirable activity changes.

Is it better for retarded children to learn in special education classrooms or with normal children? Jordan (1961) feels that this question must be answered with respect to predetermined goals. On the basis of two studies (Cassiday and Stanton, 1959; Jordan and deCharms, 1959), he concluded that special education fulfilled the responsibilities with which it was charged. This opinion was based on the results of studies which indicated that mentally retarded children placed in a school situation with normal children had a significantly higher level of achievement but poorer personality adjustment than did mentally retarded children in special classes. These findings reflected the emphasis on achievement in the normal setting as contrasted with the greater emphasis on mental hygiene in the special classes. In other words, the critical factor in determining the end results is the purpose that the teacher has in mind; the children learn what they are taught and perform to the teacher's expectations. Two studies do not yield the final answer to this question, but rather provide direction for thought.

PROGRAM AND STUDENT EVALUATION

There are apparently three levels of measurement and evaluation associated with program development: (1) screening tests, (2) evaluation of student progress toward the program objectives, and (3) school grades or marks. These three evaluations may or may not represent the same elements of measurement in general practice. The screening evaluation, which determines the student's eligibility for entry into the program, should use any medical recommendations which are available. This evaluation reflects the student's initial status and needs, and differs both from the evaluation of his progress and the assignment of grades or marks.

At this point, a distinction should be made between measurement and evaluation. Measurement refers to the determination of status; it enables one to say how things are at this time. Evaluation, on the other hand, is a more complex procedure, and requires that one determine the effectiveness with which program objectives have been met. In other words, values and priorities must be considered in order to make an evaluation. It is important to keep this distinction in mind as we are dealing with evaluation rather than measurement.

To be consistent with the definition of evaluation, all testing and appraisals must be based on the following factors:

1. *All evaluations must be related to the objectives and purposes of the physical education program.* Most programs adapted for the retarded include instruction in range-of-motion activities, functional fitness (including strength and endurance activities), motor skill development, and recreational activities. Therefore, appraisals must include measures of these aspects of the program.

2. *The evaluation should reflect the particular emphasis of the student's program.* It is impossible and often unnecessary to place equal emphasis upon all aspects of the program, such as body mechanics, activities, functional fitness, and so on. The variety of activities and emphases of the program must be considered in relation to their contribution to the individual's total program.

3. *Once the evaluative techniques have been selected, the instruments possessing the best scientific background should be used.* The evaluative devices must meet the criteria of validity, reliability, and appropriateness. Other considerations for selection would include the availability of normative data and economy of cost and administration. While normative data are beneficial in evaluation, it must be remembered that retarded students are exceptional and do not fit conveniently into norms. Consequently, norms should be used only in an advisory capacity. In some situations, the cost of a test or the amount of time required for its administration may eliminate it from use.

4. *The goals and patterns of behavior that are particularly valued by the student and the significant figures around him should be considered.* These considerations should be viewed generally as the vocational goals, social activities, and recreational patterns aspired to by the student as well as more concretely in terms of the specific physical activities or functional demands that achievement of these goals will require. The data obtained from this analysis will indicate whether he should choose physical activity or more sedentary activity as a means of expression; they will also indicate the social-emotional development of the student. There is no one best way to evaluate

these factors, although the case study approach (Clarke and Clarke, 1963) seems especially appropriate for this purpose. The teacher must rely heavily on his own skills to elicit and synthesize this information.

MOTOR PERFORMANCE AND MARKS

Marking or the assignment of grades is considered to serve the following four functions (Adams, 1965):

1. *Administrative.* The assignment of grades provides data for use in determining promotions, transfers, and graduation.

2. *Guidance.* Through the information gathered to determine grades, the teacher can identify areas of special strengths and weaknesses as a basis for appraisal of the program and future planning.

3. *Motivation.* Marks have been used to stimulate students to increased effort in order to better marks.

4. *Information.* Properly determined marks can inform students, parents, and other appropriate persons of the individual's progress toward the aims and objectives of the physical education program.

In order to fulfill the four functions of marking, any assignment of grades must be carefully considered. The specific mark must be determined by weighing the advantages and disadvantages of the evaluative procedures used. Inasmuch as evaluation takes into account the values and priorities assigned to the student's program by his instructor, the marking system must reflect the pupil's progress toward the program objectives. Such a grading procedure requires that the teacher's subjectivity of judgment be minimized as much as possible to insure that the assigned mark adequately represents the objectives and content of the physical education program.

One further essential characteristic of a good marking plan is flexibility. Such a plan allows for variations in evaluation from teacher to teacher and permits a teacher to report more fully on certain students than on others. Unfortunately, school systems using only the traditional marking system (A, B, C, D, F) do not encourage such flexibility. In these situations it is recommended that the teacher develop a supplemental form of communication that reflects the student's progress within the objectives of the physical education program.

SUMMARY

The purpose of a physical education program for mentally retarded children must be consistent with the purpose of physical education in general education. The specific objectives of a physical education program for the retarded include perceptual-motor skill development, physical fitness, social and emotional development, and the acquisition of leisure time activities.

It is critical that the program be well-planned and based on thorough instruction of small skill components in a gradual progression. The small units must be combined into larger skill units through well-organized and integrated instructional experiences. Such a program must be based upon the children's developmental level and allow for individual differences. The teacher's expectations greatly influence the children's achievement levels. Continual evaluation must be performed to determine if educational objectives are being met or if the program requires modification.

REFERENCES

Adams, G. S.: *Measurement and Evaluation in Education, Psychology and Guidance.* New York: Holt, Rinehart and Winston, 1965.

Cassiday, V. M., and Stanton, J. E.: *An Investigation of Factors Involved in the Educational Placement of Mentally Retarded Children.* Columbus: Ohio State University, 1959.

Clarke, H. Harrison, and Clarke, David H.: *Developmental and Adapted Physical Education.* Englewood Cliffs, N. J.: Prentice-Hall, 1963.

Jordan, Thomas E.: *The Mentally Retarded.* Columbus: Charles E. Merrill, 1961.

Jordan, Thomas E., and deCharms, R.: The achievement motive in normal and mentally retarded children. *Amer. J. Ment. Defic.* 64:457–466, 1959.

CHAPTER **6**

Physical Fitness

Physical fitness, a basic part of physical education programs for mentally retarded children, refers to the child's ability to carry out his daily tasks without undue fatigue and with enough energy in reserve to participate in leisure time activities and to meet unforeseen emergencies. Thus, the optimal level of physical fitness varies from person to person depending upon the life styles involved. When he is physically fit, the individual is able to withstand the stresses of life, work, recreation, and unexpected situations; moreover, physical fitness enables him to enjoy abundant life.

Researchers consider that several specific parameters constitute physical fitness. These include: (1) *muscular strength*, which is the maximum amount of effort that the muscles can exert in a single contraction; (2) *muscular endurance*, which represents the ability to persist in localized muscular effort over a period of time; (3) *circulo-respiratory endurance*, or the ability to persist in strenuous tasks involving many muscular groups for extended periods of time; and (4) *flexibility*, which is the ability to move the joints through a normal range of motion.

Other parameters that measure skill and ability, rather than physical fitness, are frequently included in various physical fitness test batteries. However, coordination, balance, power, speed, agility, and reaction time are more appropriately termed *motor ability measures*. As can be readily observed, these motor ability factors are concerned with the ability of a person to function in a coordinated manner and to move in an accurate and efficient manner. Physical fitness, on the other hand, concentrates on the person's ability to move and persist in activity rather than on the quality of his movements. A further distinction lies in the fact that a person can dramatically improve his fitness components but practice generally yields less improvement in motor performance measures.

56

ASSESSMENT OF PHYSICAL FITNESS

The assessment of physical fitness yields information that is useful in the formulation of a physical education program. This information should be used by the teacher in determining which activities are needed to improve the students' overall physical performance. Subsequent testing and evaluation will determine the amount of progress made by the students in the physical education program. Physical fitness tests used with differing groups of normal students contain items that may be appropriate for use with retarded students, but the norms do not provide useful data for the general evaluation of the retarded child's abilities.

Three physical fitness tests have been developed for use with mentally retarded children: the physical fitness test designed by Hayden (1964), the AAHPER-Kennedy Foundation Fitness Test (1968), and the Kraus-Weber Test of Minimum Muscular Fitness (Kraus and Hirschland, 1954). The Hayden and AAHPER fitness tests have norms based on the performances of mentally retarded children while the Kraus-Weber test was developed in a clinical setting and is graded only on a pass or fail basis. Table 6—1 lists the physical fitness test items according to the specific component that they measure. Items included in the test which do not measure physical fitness parameters are indicated in the footnotes. The table also contains items that are of use in determining the physical fitness status of retarded children, although they have no norms based on retarded subjects.

A key factor to remember when selecting physical fitness tests is that the components are specific. A test that measures muscular endurance of the arms will not indicate muscular strength of the arms or, muscular endurance of the trunk. Therefore, it is important that the teacher select a test that measures all components of physical fitness as well as the functioning of different body parts in each component. As indicated in Table 6.1, no single test that has been used with the retarded provides such diversity of test items. In order to obtain such information, it will be necessary to use more than one fitness test.

Since large numbers of retarded children have been unable to pass minimal standards of physical fitness, a starting point might be the initial screening of children for minimal standards of muscular strength. The Kraus-Weber Test of Minimum Muscular Fitness will indicate minimal levels of strength and flexibility for certain key muscle groups. Clinical studies suggest that if a person cannot perform at this minimal fitness level, it may be detrimental to his health. If the teacher wants to measure fitness in terms other than the minimal strength and flexibility assessed by the Kraus-Weber test, then other tests and/or other items must be used. It is recommended that this test be used only as a starting point and that other evaluations also be used by the teacher. Test manuals are available for the Hayden and the AAHPER fitness tests, so

Table 6—1. Physical Fitness Components Included in Tests Frequently Used with Mentally Retarded Children

Test	Muscular Strength	Muscular Endurance	Circulo-respiratory Endurance	Flexibility
			Physical Fitness Component	
Hayden test item[1]		Hang for time (arms)	300 yd. run	Back extension
AAHPER test items[2]		Sit-ups (abdomen)	300 yd. walk-run	
Kraus-Weber test items	Straight leg sit-ups (abdomen) Bent leg sit-ups (abdomen) Supine leg lift (abdomen) Chest raise (upper back) Prone leg lift (lower back)			Toe touch (legs & back)
Other suggested test items[3]	Lift of maximum weight Manometer grip strength	Push-ups (arms) Parallel bar dips (arms) Squat jumps (legs)	Bench stepping 600 yd. walk-run Squat thrust	Arm raise off floor

[1] The test also includes motor performance items of medicine ball throw and vertical jump which measure power (application of force over a period of time).

[2] The test also includes motor performance items of shuttle run (agility), standing broad jump (power), 50 yd. dash (speed), and softball throw for distance (power and coordination).

[3] These items are described in a number of test and measurement books. See Clarke, H. Harrison: *Application of Measurement to Health and Physical Education*, 4th ed. Englewood Cliffs, N. J.: Prentice-Hall, 1967.

their administration procedures will not be discussed. Because no manual is available for the Kraus-Weber test, the following procedures are suggested (Clarke, 1967):

1. Strength of the abdominal plus psoas muscles: The subject lies in a supine position, hands behind the neck; the examiner holds his feet down. The test is to perform one sit-up.

2. Strength of the abdominal muscles without the help of the psoas: The subject is in the same position as for number 1, except the knees are bent with the heels close to the buttocks. The test is to perform one sit-up.

3. Strength of the psoas and lower abdominal muscles: The subject is supine with hands behind the neck; the legs are fully extended with the heels 10 inches above the floor. The test is to hold this position for 10 seconds.

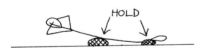

4. Strength of the upper back muscles: The subject lies prone with a pillow under the hips and lower abdomen, hands behind the neck; the examiner holds his feet down. The test is for the subject to raise his chest, head and shoulders and hold them up without touching the floor for 10 seconds.

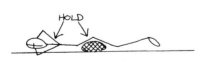

5. Strength of the lower back: The subject is in the same position as number 4, except the examiner holds his chest down. The test is for the subject to raise his legs off the table, with knees straight, and hold this position for 10 seconds.

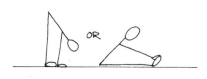

6. Length of the back and hamstring muscles. The subject stands erect, hands at his sides, feet together. The test is for the subject to lean down slowly and touch the floor with his fingertips; this position is held for 3 seconds without bouncing. The examiner should hold the knees of the person being tested in order to prevent any bend and to detect a slight bend in case it occurs.

THE PHYSICAL FITNESS PROGRAM

The basic principle underlying the development of physical fitness can best be described through the "law of use and disuse." This law states that strength and endurance increase in the muscles that are used, and decrease in muscles that are not used. Thus, a program to develop any of the physical fitness components must continually overload or subject the muscular and circulatory systems to more activity than they normally perform. There is nothing unique in activities used to develop physical fitness and any number of different types may be used. Fitness activities most commonly include specifically developed exercises, relays, games, and sports activities. Critical to success is the progressive application of overload which requires the muscular systems to perform more work in a systematic fashion. Overload of activities may be achieved in a number of ways: (1) the student can perform activities against more resistance; (2) the activity may be performed with greater intensity; (3) the activity may be performed for longer time periods; or (4) shorter rest periods may be given between activity periods. Overloading must, of course, be kept within the student's exercise tolerance and should be planned for progression. Such planning allows the pupil to extend himself more and more as his performance level improves.

Clarke and Clarke (1963) and Schurr (1967) emphasize several principles that should be used as guidelines in developing physical fitness. These principles include the following:

1. The activities must be within the student's tolerance level.

2. The overload principle must be applied to increase physical fitness.

3. The activities should be performed consistently and regularly according to a definite progression.

4. The child must be motivated to perform the activities well and to improve his status.

5. The physical fitness status of the children should be retested at set times.

6. The activities should be of a reasonable length and allow for individual differences.

Because almost any type of physical activity has the potential for developing physical fitness, a comprehensive listing would be impossible. Table 6—2 suggests categories of activities that may be used to develop specific physical fitness components. For any activity to contribute to the health and well-being of the children, it must be used in accordance with the preceding list of principles.

Table 6—2. Activities Contributing to the Development of Physical Fitness Components

	Activities
Muscular strength	Specific exercises for various muscular groups, individual stunts, self-testing activities, progressive resistance activities, obstacle course, sports, lead-up games, tumbling, and apparatus activities.
Muscular endurance	Specific exercises for various muscle groups, individual stunts, relays, combatives, mimetics, self-testing activities, progressive resistance activities, obstacle course, sports, lead-up games, tumbling, and apparatus activities.
Circulo-respiratory endurance	Walking, running, swimming, rope-jumping, cycling, hopping, individual stunts, climbing stairs, tag games, relays, soccer games, self-testing activities, obstacle course, sports, and lead-up games.
Flexibility	Specific exercises for various muscle groups, individual stunts, mimetics, self-testing activities, movement of body parts through full range of movement, obstacle course, tumbling, and apparatus activities.

Muscular Strength and Endurance

The most common activities used to develop muscular strength and endurance overload the body through resistance supplied in any of several ways. Resistance may be supplied by the body or body parts through the use of calisthenics, tumbling, or gymnastic activities. Wrestling, tug-of-war, and other types of combative activities use another individual to supply resistance. Various types of weights, most commonly barbells and medicine balls, are examples of inanimate objects that can be used for overload. These activities, when properly applied, are among the most effective methods of rapidly improving muscular strength and endurance.

Circulo-respiratory Endurance

Activities that develop circulo-respiratory endurance involve the use of the large groups of muscles for relatively long periods of time. In order to provide an overload, the activity should require some adjustment of the circulatory and respiratory systems, evidenced by an increase in pulse and breathing rates. Activities that favor the development of circulo-respiratory endurance include walking, stair-climbing, running, rope-jumping, swimming, bicycling, and the like. These activities can be well controlled and the duration, speed, distance, and type of activity should be specified in accordance with the individual's fitness status and exercise tolerance. For the less severely retarded individual, many games and sports can enhance the development of endurance. The running involved in soccer and other sports represents vigorous circulo-respiratory endurance activity.

Flexibility

Flexibility refers to the ability to move through the range of motion about a joint. Inasmuch as the degree of flexibility determines the extent of bending and stretching of a joint, it affects the child's ability to bend, twist, turn, and reach. Flexibility is highly specific to each joint, being determined by the nature of the joint itself and the condition of the ligaments and muscles related to the joint. Flexibility can best be developed by encouraging the individual to move the body parts through the full range of motion; it may be enhanced by specific exercises designed to increase the range of motion in joints or through other forms of physical activity requiring movement of joints. Walking, swimming, mimetics, obstacle courses, and sports such as basketball may increase flexibility if a full range of motion is used in the activity.

CONDITIONING EXERCISES

Conditioning exercises may be used to supplement other aspects of a physical education program and to assure balance and continuity in the development of physical fitness. When placed at the start of the physical education period they may be used for warm-up purposes. If the major part of the classwork has been devoted to mild physical activity, then these exercises may be placed at the end of the class. In any event, the conditioning exercises should be selected to fulfill a definite purpose. The following exercises were selected to provide a sample program of conditioning activities that involve the entire body and several fitness components. The specific contribution of each exercise is noted at the end of the description.

Push-ups

Assume a front-leaning rest position, supporting the body with the hands and toes. Keep the hands under the shoulders with the fingers pointed forward, arms straight, and the body kept straight. Bend the elbows and touch chest to the floor; then return to the starting position. Keep body straight throughout the movement.

For children unable to perform a regular push-up, the starting position may be modified by supporting the body weight with the hands and knees.

The knees are placed on the floor and the body is extended until it is straight from the head to the knees. The modified push-up is then executed in the same manner as a regular push-up. (For arm and shoulder muscles.)

Head and Shoulder Curl

Lie on the back with hands clasped, palms down, behind the small of the back. Slowly curling the body, lift the head, shoulders, and elbows off the floor, hold, and then return to the starting position. (For abdominal muscles.)

Sit-ups

Lie on the back with legs straight and fingers interlaced behind the neck. Sit up and touch right elbow to left knee. Return to the starting position. Sit up and touch the left elbow to the right knee. Return to the starting position. (For abdominal and lower back muscles.)

Sit-up with Bent Knees

Lie on the back with the arms crossed on the chest and knees bent at a right angle so that the feet are flat on the floor. Curl up to a sitting position; then return to the starting position. (For abdominal muscles.)

The Bouncer

Stand at attention, keeping the arms at the sides and knees straight. Bounce into the air using only ankle and calf muscles. (For lower leg muscles.)

Russian Hop

Assume a squat position with the feet together and arms folded across the chest. Leap upward off both feet and then return to the starting position. (For leg muscles.)

Riding a Bicycle

Lie flat on the back with legs and hips raised, elbows on the floor, supporting the hips with both hands. Move the legs vigorously, as though pedaling a bike, bringing the knees close to the chest. (For leg and hip muscles.)

Back Leg and Arm Raises

Lie face down with arms extended in front of the head. Alternately raise and lower legs, keeping the knees straight; then alternately raise and lower the arms. This exercise may be made more difficult by raising both the arms and legs simultaneously. (For back muscles.)

Toe Toucher

Start from a standing position with the arms extended above the head. Bend the body forward and down, keeping the knees straight, and touch the fingers to the toes. Return to the starting position. (For flexibility.)

Windmill

Start from a standing position with the feet spread shoulder-width apart and the arms extended sideward at shoulder height. Twist and bend the trunk, touching right hand to left toe, keeping the arms and legs straight. Return to the starting position. Then twist and bend the trunk to the other side, touching the left hand to the right toe. (For flexibility.)

Squat Thrust

Starting from a standing position, bend the knees and place the hands on the floor in front of the feet (squat position). Thrust the legs back far enough so that the body is perfectly straight from the shoulders to the feet (push-up position). Return to the squat position, and then to the standing position. (For general body movement and endurance.)

Prancing Horses

Run in place at various speeds, pumping the arms, raising the knees high and landing on the balls of the feet. (For circulo-respiratory endurance.)

SUMMARY

The development and maintenance of an adequate level of physical fitness is essential to good health. Physical fitness is the ability of an individual to carry out his daily tasks while maintaining an energy reserve for leisure activities and unexpected situations. Physical fitness is not a single characteristic, but comprises muscular strength, muscular endurance, circulo-respiratory endurance, and flexibility.

The development of physical fitness must be based on an adequate testing program. Initial testing is necessary to determine the individual's status and needs while subsequent testing will indicate the success of the program. Certain types of activities are applicable to the development of the various fitness components, but each program should be developed in accordance with the recognized principles of exercise tolerance and overload.

REFERENCES

Adult Physical Fitness: A Program for Men and Women. Washington, D.C.: U.S. Government Printing Office, 1963.

Bender, Jay, and Shea, Edward J.: *Physical Fitness: Tests and Exercises.* New York: Ronald Press, 1964.

Clarke, H. Harrison: *Application of Measurement to Health and Physical Education.* Englewood Cliffs, N.J.: Prentice-Hall, 1967.

Clarke, H. Harrison, and Clarke, David H.: *Developmental and Adapted Physical Education.* Englewood Cliffs, N.J.: Prentice-Hall, 1967.

Hayden, Frank J.: *Physical Fitness for the Mentally Retarded.* Toronto, Ontario, Canada: Metropolitan Toronto Association for Retarded Children, 1964.

Kraus, Hans, and Hirschland, Ruth P.: Minimum muscular fitness tests in school children. *Research Quarterly,* 25:178, 1954.

Murray, Jim, and Karpovich, Peter V.: *Weight Training in Athletics.* Englewood Cliffs, N.J.: Prentice-Hall, 1956.

Physical Conditioning: TM 21-200. Washington, D.C.: U.S. Government Printing Office, 1957.

Schurr, Evelyn L.: *Movement Experiences for Children: Curriculum and Methods for Elementary School Physical Education.* New York: Appleton-Century-Crofts, 1967.

Special Fitness Test Manual for the Mentally Retarded. Washington, D.C.: American Association for Health, Physical Education and Recreation, 1968.

Youth Physical Fitness: Suggested Elements of a School-centered Program. Washington, D.C.: U.S. Government Printing Office, 1961.

CHAPTER **7**

Basic Movement Skills

One of the more important objectives of physical education for the mentally retarded is the improvement of their basic movement skills. These include abilities such as walking, running, jumping, hopping, skipping, catching, throwing, striking, and the like. Earlier in this book it was noted that the retarded child's motor skills are not as well developed as the normal child's. Since the most important factor determining the retardate's success on a motor skill is the task complexity, the more complex the task and the more learning that is required, the worse the performance of mentally retarded children. In basic movement skills which include both simple and complex activities, retarded children have varying degrees of success.

The child becomes aware of his potential and physical limitations through the development of basic skills and their use in a variety of situations. The intent of basic skill instruction is to aid the retarded child to both grasp the principles that govern movement and apply these to new motor skill problems. This basic skill instruction forms the foundation for the teaching of work skills and various leisure time pursuits vital to the retardate throughout his life.

ANALYSIS OF BASIC MOVEMENT SKILLS

This chapter is concerned with analysis and description of the basic movement skills that are critical to the child's motor performance. The descriptions may be too detailed for the retarded child to understand, but they should help the teacher gain an understanding of the movement patterns involved. The teacher should use these principles to develop instructions that are compatible with the students' developmental and comprehension levels. There are many applications for these basic movement skills; the student should be encouraged to use them in a wide variety of situations while developing competency.

66

The repertoire of skills possessed by each person, retarded or normal, is extensive. Some skills are acquired through extensive learning procedures while other innate ones are the product of developing reflexes and maturation. Most of our responses are a complex combination of learned and maturational skills. The basic movement skills are no exception.

Two methods are suggested for teaching the basic skills described here. The first involves the use of imitation learning. Although very little is known about this phenomenon, it is evident that children imitate other children and adults. If imitation is to be used an an instructional tool, the child must be taught how to imitate and must be reinforced in his imitation. The teacher is advised to observe common sense rules to reduce the necessary maneuvers to a minimum, not to expect complex tasks to be imitated, and to orient the student to the specific aspects of the task involved. The teacher's greatest difficulty may be in reducing the number of extraneous cues and emphasizing the important cues adequately.

The second method for teaching basic skills requires that the child be placed in a situation where he must perform the task correctly. The situation may be created by placing barriers or artificial restraints to eliminate undesirable skills, developing activities that dictate the correct performance of a task, or the use of games that enforce the desired skills. The following sections analyze the basic movement skills and describe activities useful in developing them.

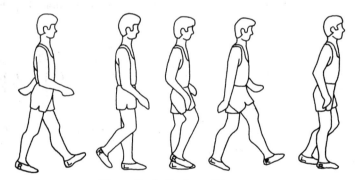

Figure 7—1. Basic walking pattern.

Walking

Walking has been described as a process of continually losing and regaining one's balance. Although locomotion is an individual matter with each person selecting the style and speed best suited to him, there are some features of walking that merit special attention.

The movement of the legs begins with a push-off as the hip flexes and the thigh starts to move forward. This motion is continued as the knee and ankle also flex to lift the foot off the ground. After the foot clears the ground under the body, the lower leg is extended and the extremity is prepared to contact the ground again. The body weight is transferred from the heel along the outer edge of the foot to the ball and finally to the toes for the next push off. The arm motion is coordinated with the legs as they swing freely in opposition to the legs as a counterbalance to the rotation of the trunk and as an aid in moving the upper part of the body forward. The unique characteristic of walking lies in the fact that both feet are simultaneously in contact with the floor for brief periods of time.

Key points in walking instruction:
1. Push off the ground with toes.
2. Swing the leg from hip, flexing hip and knee.
3. Land on heel of foot and let weight transfer along the outside edge of the foot to toes.
4. Point the toes straight ahead keeping feet parallel.
5. Keep the head up and look straight ahead.
6. Swing the arms in opposition to legs naturally.

Activities that may be used to facilitate instruction in walking include the following: walking on painted footprints; stepping over ropes or other obstacles placed on the floor; stepping between the rungs of a ladder; and, a combination of these activities such as stepping from one footprint to another over bricks that are placed between them. Activities such as walking on footprints or a wide line should be used when the feet are spread too far apart while walking; the obstacles or ladder should be used when the child drags his feet.

Figure 7–2. Basic running pattern.

Running

Running is characterized by a period of non-support during each step. After starting the stride in a manner similar to the walking step, the foot contacts the ground under the center of gravity with the weight falling on the ball of the foot. The knees, flexed more than when walking, are drawn further upward and more forward. The arm swing during the run becomes much more vigorous and the elbows are bent. Although there is no optimal speed of running, the length of the stride and the rate will affect an individual's running efficiency. It must be recognized that, inasmuch as running speed can vary from a slow jog to fast sprinting, considerable variation in the mechanical patterns observed at different speeds will occur.

Key points in running instruction:

1. Run on the ball of the foot.
2. Push off the ground with more force and lift the knees higher than in the walk.
3. Bend the elbows and swing the arms vigorously in opposition to the legs.
4. Keep the feet parallel and the head up.

Running technique may be improved by placing the child in situations that require the proper movement. For example, if the child does not lift his legs high enough or bend the knees properly, the teacher may prescribe lifting the knees high while running in place. Similarly, imaginative movements and imitation of animals, objects, or sports skills may be used to emphasize desired movements. If the child has difficulty in changing directions during a run, the tasks required may be running through or around obstacles, running under ropes, dodging obstacles or people, and following a leader who runs in an irregular pathway.

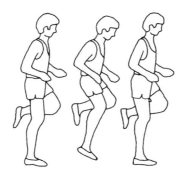

Figure 7—3. Hopping on one foot.

Hopping

The hopping movement consists of pushing the body off the floor with one foot and taking the weight on the same foot after it returns to the floor. The inactive foot is kept from contact with the floor by bending the knee. The arms are either held out from the sides to assist with balance or moved up and down to help with body lift. On landing, the weight is on the toes of the foot and may be shifted immediately to the ball of the foot and then the heel. Hopping may also be performed by pushing off with both feet simultaneously and landing on both feet. The general technique using both feet is the same as previously described.

Key points in hopping instruction:
1. Push the body up with one foot and catch the weight with the same foot.
2. Balance the body with arms out from the sides.
3. Lift the foot of nonsupporting leg by bending the knee.
4. Keep toes of the supporting foot pointing straight ahead.
5. Keep the head and body erect.

Hopping on one foot initially requires balancing on one foot. Once the child is able to perform this balance, he is asked to balance and jump over a low object (such as a rope or painted line). As his proficiency increases, he is instructed to land on the same foot as the one used to take-off and balance briefly. Once this task is mastered, the child is directed to perform several of these "hops" in serial order. The obstacles may then be removed and the child instructed to hop without aid.

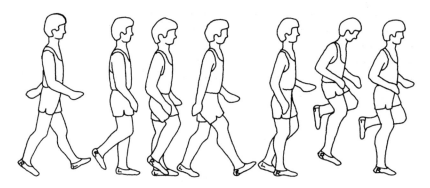

Figure 7—4. Basic skipping pattern.

Skipping

Skipping combines the step in walking with a hop. Skipping is executed by stepping forward with one foot and then hopping once on the same foot. The child then steps forward on the opposite foot and hops on it. The arms swing in opposition to the leg movement to maintain balance and gain height. The skip may be performed at a variety of speeds and in a variety of directions. In fact, this step-hop combination may be used in rhythms and dances as well as in sports skills.

Key points in skipping instruction:
1. Step forward and then hop up with the same foot.
2. Maintain balance and obtain height by swinging the arms.
3. Use alternate feet to take body weight.

Inasmuch as skipping requires the combination of two other basic movements, the step and the hop, it is one of the more difficult locomotor patterns for retarded children to learn. It is important that the child is proficient in both the step and hop before attempting the skip. Children may be aided to skip by the use of footprints in color-coded patterns, by having the child make an exaggerated arm swing up on the hop, or by taking the child's hand and skipping with him. After the skipping pattern has been mastered, music may be played while students skip in patterns alone or with partners.

Figure 7–5. Jumping and landing.

Jumping

Jumping is a movement used to propel the body either vertically up into the air or horizontally through the air. The child may take off for jumping from either foot or both feet simultaneously. In either case, the power for this movement results from a quick extension of the leg extensor muscles and a vigorous fling of the arms in the desired direction of movement. The child should crouch in a preparatory position with bent hips, knees, and ankles to achieve maximum height or distance.

When the jump is to be executed in a horizontal direction for distance, the child leans his body forward and swings his arms in the desired direction. The optimal take-off angle is approximately 45 degrees. If vertical height is the objective, the push-off is straight up, the arms are thrown upward, and the body should be extended or stretched upward as much as possible.

Key points in jumping instruction:

1. Start from a crouched position.
2. Push off the ground with a vigorous extension of the legs.
3. Throw the arms vigorously in the desired direction of movement.
4. Forward body lean should be used when jumping for horizontal distance.

Jumping skills can be acquired only after success in a complex learning situation, so more severely retarded children may have difficulty with jumping tasks. Many retarded children have difficulty using both feet simultaneously during the jump. Several methods may be successful in teaching the jump. A rope, some sticks, or piece of cloth may be placed on the floor and the child instructed to jump over them. Painted lines or colored tape placed at varying distances on the floor will frequently motivate the child to improve horizontal jumping distances. Some children who experience difficulty in getting both feet off the ground improve when placed on a flexible surface (such as a trampoline or elevated flexible board) when jumping. Frequently the teacher may have to hold the child's hands and assist him during the jump.

After the jumping skill has been successfully acquired, the child should be encouraged to use it in a variety of situations. For example, he may jump sidewards, backwards, down from boxes, and up onto objects as well as forwards. He may jump and turn or jump and balance. Targets may be used to encourage height in a vertical jump or distance in a horizontal jump. Jumping rope is an excellent activity to further improve jumping skills.

Landing

Understanding the proper way to land after jumping for height or distance is an important safety skill. Relaxing the legs and bending the knees and ankles should provide some "give" as contact is made with the ground. This "give" allows for the time and distance in which speed is reduced and body weight is absorbed. After the landing has been completed, the legs may be extended and the body returned to the starting position. The arms may be extended from the sides of the body to assist with balance (see Figure 7–5).

It is strongly recommended that a level landing surface be used when teaching jumping and landing. Uneven surfaces may throw the child's weight to the side and cause severe knee injuries or ankle sprains.

Key points in landing instruction:
1. Land on the balls of the feet with bent knees.
2. Give or relax with the movement to absorb the landing force.
3. Extend the arms sidewards for balance.

Every jump must be accompanied by a landing, and any sports skill or dance movement that takes the body into the air requires a landing. Thus landing should be taught simultaneously with jumping. The activities mentioned for use with jumping instruction may also be used with landing. Other tasks stressing proper landing techniques include a jump into the air with a landing followed by an immediate rebound into the air, and a jump and landing that is preceded by and followed by another type of movement. Imitating animals may also help the child learn to jump and land correctly.

Throwing

The many different styles of throwing depend upon the size of the ball used, the distance and speed desired from the ball, and the game in which the

Figure 7–6. Single overarm throw.

throw is being used. The basic principles essential to success for all throwing patterns are similar. The speed imparted to the ball depends on the backswing, stance, transfer of body weight and follow through. Distance is controlled by the speed of the ball at the time it is released and the angle at which it is released. Direction, of course, is influenced by the direction that the hand is moving when the ball is released. Two styles of throwing, the single underarm throw and the single overarm throw will be discussed here.

Single Underarm Throw. An understanding of this throw is particularly important as the child's first throwing attempt is usually the two-hand underarm toss. The single underarm throw develops from the beginner's two-hand underarm toss. The throw begins with the thrower facing the target with his feet together. The throwing arm is drawn straight back and down. Simultaneously, the body is rotated slightly toward the throwing arm and the weight is shifted to the same foot. Next the throwing arm is rapidly swung forward at the same time a step forward is taken with the opposite foot. The ball is released as the fingers are straightened slightly to allow the ball to roll off them at the bottom of the arc described by the hand (i.e., when the arm is at a right angle to the direction the ball will travel). The throwing arm continues somewhat higher in a follow through, while the other arm swings easily backward in opposition.

Key points in underarm throw instruction:
1. Start the throw facing the target with feet together.
2. Bring the throwing arm back and turn the body toward that side.
3. Swing the throwing arm forward and step forward with the opposite leg.
4. Release the ball at the bottom of the throwing arc.
5. Follow through with the throwing arm.

Single Overarm Throw. The following describes a right-handed throw; the technique is reversed for a left-handed person. The preparatory position for this action requires the thrower to stand in a stride position with the left side facing the target. The ball is grasped in the fingers and the right arm is raised with the elbow bent about shoulder height. The backswing begins when the arm is brought backward past the shoulder and away from the body; the elbow may or may not be extended. The left arm is raised for balance and pointed toward the target. The throw is made by a quick reversal in all directions; the elbow is brought forward with the hand trailing, the wrist and hand snap forward and the ball is released when the hand is just in front of the shoulder. As this forward motion is made, the trunk rotates toward the target and the body weight shifts to the left foot. The throwing hand and arm continue their motion toward the target for the follow through and a step may be taken with the right foot to regain balance and prepare for another movement.

Key points in overarm throw instruction:
1. Keep eyes on the target.
2. Point the left side of the body toward the target.
3. Bring the right arm back and behind the shoulder.
4. Lead with the elbow and release the ball in front of the shoulder.
5. Transfer weight from the right foot to the left foot during the throw.
6. Follow through with the right arm.

The key to teaching either the single underarm or overarm throw is the selection of the throwing object. Inasmuch as these throws are primarily used with objects small enough to be held by the fingers, objects such as beanbags, fleece balls, or tennis balls should be used. Large darts with rubber suction grippers or similar objects may also be used with success. The children stand close to a wall and throw at it, while the teacher emphasizes proper throwing pattern rather than distance or accuracy. As throwing ability increases, the children may move back from the wall, targets may be added, and different sized balls may be used. If a two-hand underarm throw is desired, use a ball that is large enough to require the support of the child's non-throwing arm on the backswing.

Figure 7—7. Catching a ball.

Catching

It is essential that the child watch the motion of the ball in order to position himself properly to catch it. He should be in line with, directly behind, or underneath the ball before attempting to make the catch. In order to stop the ball, the arms and body must relax or give during the catch to allow the time and space necessary to reduce the velocity of the ball. Without this give, the ball will rebound from the hands and a catch would be almost impossible. The fingers are spread and slightly curved and the feet placed in a forward stride position. If the ball is to be received above the waist, the hands are held with the thumbs together and the fingers pointing upward; if the ball will be caught below the waist, the hands are held with the little fingers together and the rest of the fingers pointing downward.

Key points in catching instruction:
1. Watch the ball come into your hands.
2. Keep your body in line with the ball.
3. Spread the fingers and give with the ball.
4. To catch below the waist, fingers point downward; above the waist, fingers point upward.
5. Keep the feet spread apart.

The proper selection of objects to be caught and the progression followed during instruction may determine the child's success in catching. The object used should be soft, light-weight, and not lively. A properly inflated rubber playground ball is too difficult to catch because of its extreme bounce. A beanbag, fleece ball, or cloth-stuffed ball is recommended for initial instruction. The progression should begin with the child throwing the object to himself and catching it. Later he may throw a ball against a wall or bounce it on the floor and catch it. Once the proper catching technique is used, he may catch balls thrown by a partner or attempt to catch balls of varying weight, size, and bounce characteristics.

Figure 7–8. Basic striking pattern.

Striking

The striking movement is used in a wide variety of sports and work skills. The striking implement may be the hand, foot, or tools such as bats, paddles, rackets, clubs, hammers or the like. Regardless of the implement, the principles are the same, and are similar to those involved in throwing.

The performer attempts to carry the striking implement through as long an arc as can be properly controlled in the least amount of time. The amount of momentum developed will depend upon the length of the backswing, the length and firmness of the tool, the number of muscles involved, and their coordination during the movement. The object should be struck at the instant the maximum speed of the swing has been reached. The direction that the ball (or object that has been hit) will travel is determined by the direction of the striking surface at the instant of contact. The feet are spread in a stance that provides a solid base, particularly when fast-moving objects are to be struck and propelled any distance. After the object has been contacted, the swing should be continued to provide a follow through for the action. If the hand or foot is used as the striking tool, the broadest, firmest parts should be used as the striking surface. A good firm grip should be maintained on all other striking implements.

Key points in striking instruction:
1. Keep your eyes on the object to be hit.
2. Spread your feet to make a solid base.
3. Use a long, level swing.
4. Transfer your weight from back foot to forward foot.
5. Strike just below the center of the object.
6. Follow through in the direction of the target.

The striking pattern should be practiced in a variety of situations both with and without implements. Balloons may be hit with the hands, kicked with the feet, or struck with a variety of implements. To keep the balloon from bouncing a great deal, place a small amount of water inside before inflating it. Playground balls or volleyballs may be used in the same manner. A number of commercially produced games made from plastic are also useful in teaching the striking patterns.

Teaching progression should follow these general principles: (1) begin with large objects and move to smaller ones as skill increases; (2) begin with stationary objects and positions, progressing to moving ones after skill is developed; (3) have the students work alone until they are skilled enough to have success with others; (4) use relays and games only after sufficient skill levels are developed, *not* before.

Pushing

Pushing may take place in any plane of motion and apply to any type of object. It is a forceful movement that is made to move some object away from the body or to move the body away from it. If the object is light, a push may involve only a hand or an arm, while moving a heavy object may involve a combination of many body parts. With very heavy objects, for example, the knees are flexed so that leg extension can be added to arm extension. The pushing motion consists of the preparatory bend or flexion followed by a forceful extension to move the object.

Key points in pushing instruction:

1. Line the body up with the direction of the push.
2. Keep the center of gravity low.
3. Keep your feet parallel with one foot slightly ahead of the other.
4. Flex the body or body parts and push with extension.

Objects used to teach the correct method of pushing should have varying degrees of resistance to movement. Wagons and other toys with wheels provide little resistance while boxes of differing weights provide more resistance. Pushing in a horizontal plane is easier than pushing up an inclined plane. Instruction should begin with objects providing little resistance being moved in a horizontal plane; later instruction should include objects with increased resistance moved in inclined planes.

Pulling

Pulling is similar to pushing in many respects except that an object is drawn toward the body or the body may be drawn toward it. Most often pulling involves only the arms, but leg extension and a body lean may be used with heavy resistance. The pull begins with the arms extended, then the object is drawn toward the body as the elbows and wrists flex. A stable stance with the feet spread should be used.

Key points in pulling instruction:

1. Line the body up with the direction of the pull.
2. Use a stable stance with the feet spread and the center of gravity lowered.
3. Pull the object toward the body as the arms move from extension to flexion.

Objects and situations that are similar to those described for pushing may be used to teach pulling. In addition to the use of objects and planes of movement, self-testing stunts such as tug-of-war games may be employed. Mild, well-supervised combative games involving two students standing face to face or back to back and attempting to pull each other to designated areas offer excellent situations to use pulling patterns and are well received by the children.

Lifting

Lifting is a form of pulling which involves raising an object or body part from one level to another; it usually incorporates the use of the legs and other body parts. One should stand close beside the object to be raised, flex the knees, and grasp the object with arms extended. Lifting is then a combination of extending the legs and flexing the arms. For ease in maintaining balance and economy of effort, the object should be kept near the body and the feet should be spread to provide a stable base. If the object is to be carried once it has been lifted, it should be kept near the body for ease in handling. If the object sways or moves, it becomes much more difficult to lift or carry.

Figure 7–9. Basic lifting pattern.

Key points in lifting instruction:
1. Stand close to the object and bend the knees.
2. Lift by extending the legs and, if necessary, bending the arms.
3. Keep the back erect.
4. Never stoop over from the waist.
5. Keep the object near the body as it is lifted or carried.

Lifting instruction should begin with objects that are easy to manage in terms of both size and weight. Large toy building bricks made from cardboard or wood are good examples of usable objects. After the principles are mastered, large, bulky objects of increased weight may be used. Lifting instruction may be included in the physical fitness aspects of the program or as a separate unit of instruction. Mimicking the activities of weightlifters or brick masons may also aid in teaching children how to lift properly.

SUMMARY

It is necessary that basic movement skills be taught to retarded children in easily-grasped units of their component parts. When adequately mastered they form the basis of the more complex skills needed for social, recreational, and vocational achievement.

The fundamental skills of walking, running, hopping, skipping, jumping, landing, throwing, catching, striking, pushing, pulling, and lifting are described briefly, along with a listing of key points for use by the teacher.

REFERENCES

Godfrey, Barbara B., and Kephart, Newell C.: *Movement Patterns and Motor Education.* New York: Appleton-Century-Crofts, 1969.

Latchaw, Marjorie: *A Pocket Guide of Movement Activities for the Elementary School*, 2nd ed. Englewood Cliffs, N.J.: Prentice-Hall, 1970.

Latchaw, Marjorie, and Egstrom, Glen: *Human Movement with Concepts Applied to Children's Movement Activities*. Englewood Cliffs, N.J.: Prentice-Hall, 1969.

Mosston, Muska: *Developmental Movement*. Columbus, Ohio: Charles E. Merrill, 1965.

Schurr, Evelyn L.: *Movement Experiences for Children: Curriculum and Methods for Elementary School Physical Education*. New York: Appleton-Century-Crofts, 1967.

Scott, M. Gladys: *Analysis of Human Motion: A Textbook in Kinesiology*, 2nd ed. New York: Appleton-Century-Crofts, 1963.

Wickstrom, Ralph L.: *Fundamental Motor Patterns*. Philadelphia: Lea & Febiger, 1970.

CHAPTER **8**

Perceptual-Motor Development

The development of perceptual-motor behavior requires the interaction of two important physiological systems: the sensory system, which provides information about the environment, and the motor or muscular system, which allows the organism to respond to its environment. The meshing of these two systems and the development of perceptions and concepts is necessary for a higher-order learning process. Only after perceptions have been developed does the individual develop a sense of stability about his environment. Thus, activities that assist in perceptual-motor development are vital to physical education programs for the retarded.

The basic question of how the child develops perceptions has been investigated by many researchers. Kephart (1964) believes that the child's motor interactions with his environment are critical to his development. He places particular importance on the development of four broad motor patterns which he distinguishes from skills in that they have less precision and greater variability. These critical patterns are defined by Kephart as balance and the maintenance of posture, locomotive skills that move the body through space, contact skills that allow the child to manipulate objects, and receipt and propulsion skills that enable the child to make contact with moving objects and to impart movement to objects. It is through these motor patterns that the child is able to explore and learn about his environment.

Other investigators have also noted the importance of motor activity in the development of perceptions. After intensive study, Piaget (1967) reported three periods of sensorimotor development. The first period is characterized by the development of the perceptions of proximity, separation, order (spatial succession), enclosure or surrounding, and continuity. During the second period of development vision is coordinated with grasping and manipulation, resulting in the development of size and shape constancy. In the third period of development, the child learns through systematic observation of, and experimentation in, the environment. Piaget thus concurs that the child's development of perception is almost entirely the product of an interaction of the sensory and motor systems.

Although the first two periods of development pass rather naturally and rapidly for the normal child, these processes may be an entirely different matter for the retarded. Frequently these perceptions are learned only through a systematic, well-designed program of instruction.

Many investigators (Fleishman, 1954 and 1957; Fleishman and Hempel, 1954 and 1956; Guilford, 1958; Cumbee, 1954; Cumbee *et al.*, 1957) have attempted to determine which factors make up perceptual-motor ability; in some cases elaborate theories of movement have resulted (Smith and Smith, 1962). However, the results of these studies may be consolidated into four primary components of perceptual-motor behavior: balance, coordination, sensorimotor perception, and speed of movement. Activities that contribute to the development of these components will be described in detail.

BALANCE

The development of a sense of balance is basic to all motor patterns. Even locomotion and erect posture are impossible for the individual who is unable to develop balance and concomitant postural control. Once adequate balance is achieved, active exploration of the environment can begin. Balance mechanisms are used continually in static postures such as standing, and in dynamic postures such as running. The semi-circular canals of the ears, as well as other visual, tactual, and kinesthetic receptors, all supply information that is important in maintaining balance.

Through the development of balance, the child learns to relate to the force of gravity and begins to formulate a reference system. He learns principles of stability, and uses his center of gravity as a reference point around which to develop the concepts of up-down, right-left, and front-back. That principles of stability must be learned is evident to the parent or teacher when they observe a child with poor balance walking with his feet spread wide apart. The maintenance of balance yields accurate knowledge, or inner awareness, of the differences between the two sides of the body and their relationship to each other, enabling the child to adjust his balance by raising or lowering one arm relative to the other.

Early investigators (Seashore, 1947; Bass, 1939; Travis, 1945) hypothesized two types of balance, static and dynamic. However, Drowatzky and Zuccato (1967) indicated that balance is a highly specific factor that differs from situation to situation, and they suggest that the teacher expose the child to a variety of balance activities. Although physical education programs require varied balance problems to be effective, the teacher should evaluate the difficulty of the items used in terms of the following principles of stability:

1. The larger the area of the base of support, the more stable the child will be. This principle is related to the second.

2. The lower the location of the center of gravity, the more stable a person will be. If the size of the base is increased while the height of the person remains the same, the center of gravity will be lowered. Conversely, a decrease in the area of the base raises the center of gravity, all other things remaining equal.

3. A person is more stable when the center of gravity is located close to the center of the base of support.

4. A stationary person is more stable than a person who is moving, all other things being equal.

5. The heavier an object, all other things being equal, the greater the stability.

The teacher must consider the first four principles of stability to create situations requiring different degrees of skill in balance. Thus, different situations will be obtained if the teacher directs the child to perform movements or assume positions that cause changes in the size of the base, the location of the center of gravity or the amount of movement required. Further, the teacher may make the balancing act more difficult by reducing the sensory information going to the brain, by closing the eyes and eliminating visual feedback, for example. The following balance activities, suggested for use in a development program, include static and dynamic balance tasks; directions to build any needed equipment are given in Chapter 12. In order to achieve progression in terms of difficulty, recall that a position using three points of support is less stable than one with four, two points of support are less stable than three, and so on.

Balance Stunts and Activities Requiring No Equipment

It is important for the teacher to remain near the children and to assist them with the support they may need as they attempt new activities. In the first series of activities, the child assumes the basic position of kneeling on his hands and knees.

1. In the basic position, raise one arm and move it about; return to starting position, raise the other arm, and repeat the action.

2. Raise one leg and kick it; return to starting position, raise the other leg, and repeat the action.

3. Raise one arm and the opposite leg; return to starting position and repeat with other arm and leg.

4. Raise arm and leg on same side of the body; return to starting position and repeat using other arm and leg.

5. Repeat this sequence, supporting the body on hands and toes.

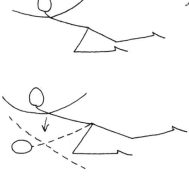

✳6. *Knee scale*: Kneeling on one knee, raise the other leg from the floor and stretch both arms out at shoulder level. Repeat with the other knee.

7. *Dynamic knee scale*: Assuming the same balance position as above, bend trunk forward, touch nose to floor in front of the knee supporting body weight, and resume the balance position. (Note: It is important that this stunt be done on a gymnastic mat and that the student be spotted.)

Although the next series varies in difficulty, each stunt may be made more difficult by requiring the student to close his eyes while performing. The teacher should support the child while he is learning these skills.

✳1. Stand with one foot directly in front of the other, heel to toe with the feet making a straight line.

✳2. Stand with the heels of both feet together and the toes pointing out sidewards.

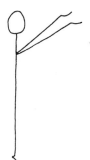

3. *Diver's stand*: Stand on the toes with heels together; stretch arms out straight at shoulder level. This stunt is considerably more difficult when the eyes are closed.

✳4. *One foot stand*: Stand on one foot using arms to balance. This stunt may be made progressively more difficult by placing the hands behind the neck or on the head, balancing on tiptoe, and closing the eyes.

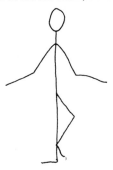

✳5. *Stork stand*: Balance on the left foot while holding the bottom of the right foot against the inside of the left knee. This stunt may be made more difficult by placing the hands on the hips. Repeat action while balanced on other foot.

4

6. *Stepping stones or island hopping:* Paint or place forms cut from some nonskid material on the floor in the desired pattern and direct the child to hop from stone to stone, using the same or alternate legs for each hop.

7. *Stand from knees:* Kneel on both knees with arms folded across the chest. Stand up without losing balance or moving feet from their spot on the floor.

8. *Balance and hop:* Balancing on one foot, hop forward without losing balance. Repeat with one hop backwards; hop with ¼ turn right or left.

9. *Jump and turn:* Standing with both feet together, jump from the floor with a ½ turn right or left without losing balance. Requiring ¾ or full turn makes the exercise more difficult.

10. *One foot balance with head touch:* Balancing on one foot, bend the trunk forward, place both hands on the floor, touch forehead to the floor. Regain one foot balance.

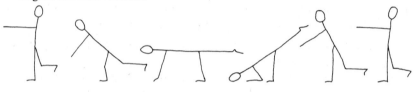

11. *Single leg squat:* Balance on one foot with the other leg extended in front of the body. Bend knee to sit on that foot and regain balance.

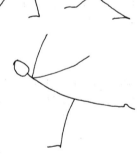

12. *Front scale:* From a standing position, slowly lean forward so that the upper body lowers to a position parallel to the floor; at the same time, elevate one leg to make a straight line with the chest that is also parallel to the floor. The arms are held in a swan position; the head is up and the back arched.

13. *Side scale:* This same type of scale can be done to the side by leaning to the right and lifting the left leg. The right arm is placed close to the head and then extended out to the right with left arm along the body down towards the knee. The scale may be done on the other side of the body.

14. *Balance seat:* Sitting on the floor, lift both legs and hold outstretched without bending the knees. The body assumes a V-position. The hands may be on the floor behind the student, or stretched out at shoulder height to increase the difficulty.

Balance Beam Stunts and Activities

It may be necessary, in some cases, to start the handicapped child on balance beam work activities by walking on a line painted on the floor. The child would progress to a 2 x 4 board placed on its side on the floor. After the student has mastered this equipment, the balancing task may be made more difficult by raising the board off the floor, decreasing its width, or increasing the difficulty of the stunt. The following activities are effective when performed on a balance beam. Note that the child may watch his feet only at the start of instruction; after the initial period of adjustment he should look straight ahead.

1. Walk forward across the balance beam, eyes fixed on a target placed at eye level.

2. Walk backward across the beam, keeping the eyes on the target. Walk naturally or in a toe-heel fashion.

3. Walk forward across the beam, keeping the right foot in front of the left foot.

4. Walk forward across the beam, keeping the left foot in front of the right foot.

5. Walk sideward across the beam, leading with the right foot.

6. Walk sideward across the beam, leading with the left foot.

7. Walk forward across the beam carrying a weight first in the right, then in the left hand.

8. Walk forward across the beam, transferring the weight from hand to hand. Repeat while walking backward.

9. Walk backward across the beam with the left foot in front of the right; then with the right foot in front of the left.

10. Walk forward while balancing a light object on one hand. Repeat with the object on the other hand. Walk backward, balacing object first on one hand, then on the other.

11. Walk forward and backward across the beam with a light object balanced on the head.

12. Walk across the beam, throwing a bean bag, or small ball at a target on command.

13. Walk across the beam, catching and throwing a bean bag or small ball to the teacher.

14. Walk across the beam while bouncing a ball on the floor. Repeat with the other hand and in the opposite direction.

15. Walk forward to the middle of the beam, turn around and walk the rest of the beam backward.

16. Walk forward across the beam, pick up an eraser or bean bag, and return to the starting point walking backward.

17. Place boxes or similar objects on the beam. Walk forward across the beam stepping over the objects.

18. Walk forward across the beam, stepping over a wand or rope held at varying heights above the beam.

19. Walk forward to the center of the beam, balance on one foot, and walk backward to the starting point.

20. Walk to the center of the beam, squat, return to a standing position and walk to the end of the beam.

21. Walk the beam in both directions on tiptoe.

22. Walk forward across the beam and pass under a wand held about 3 feet above the beam.

23. Walk forward across the beam, balancing a light object in the palm of each hand.

24. Walk to the center of the board, kneel on one knee (knee scale), return to a standing position and walk to the end of the board.

25. Have the children invent new ways to cross the board.

Other Balance Equipment and Activities

The balance board and the rocking board present other opportunities for the child to acquire balance skills. Besides learning to balance himself on these boards, the child may also catch or bounce balls while balanced. He may twist while on the balance board or rock under control on the rocking board. These activities become more difficult if the child closes his eyes. Be sure to spot the child in order to avoid a fall or injury while he learns to work with this equipment.

Stilts are a challenging piece of equipment when used in teaching balance skills. The difficulty varies with the height and bases of the stilts. Various stunts that may be performed while standing on stilts provide a further challenge. Note that it is easier to stand than to walk rapidly and easier to walk in a straight line rather than to change directions.

COORDINATION

Coordination refers to the ability to combine many muscular movements into a smoothly unified pattern of movement. A well-coordinated person is able to move in a smooth series of combined movements and to perform a complex unitary movement efficiently. Agility, which is part of coordination, enables the individual to change direction quickly and accurately. Coordination requires not only the proper sequential arrangement of muscular movements, but also the proper timing (duration of activity) and rhythm (regularity of movements).

Balance is an important factor underlying coordination, but the individual must also make rapid adaptive decisions based on his judgments of time, height, distance, and direction. Since good coordination requires movements in all patterns and directions, physical education programs should include a variety of movement patterns and directions. The retarded child should be encouraged to try a number of simple stunts and activities rather than attempt a few more complex movements. The following activities may be used in addition to the basic exercises for the development of coordination through the basic skills of movement described in Chapter 7.

Developmental Activities for Coordination

1. *Walk on all fours:* Bending over at the waist, place hands on the floor and walk forward on hands and feet.

2. *Bear walk:* Bend forward in position to walk on all fours. Travel forward by moving first the right arm and right leg together and then the left arm and left leg.

3. *Elephant walk:* Bend forward in position to walk on all fours. Walk forward keeping knees and elbows stiff and the hips elevated. Variation: Bend forward at the waist and allow the arms to hang limp, hands clasped. Walk with big, lumbering steps, swaying from side to side imitating an elephant.

4. *Lame dog walk:* Walk on both hands and one foot. Hold the other leg high in the air, imitating a dog with a sore foot.

5. *Bunny hop:* Raise the hands to the side of the head to form bunny ears. Hop on both feet simultaneously, wiggling the ears by moving the hands.

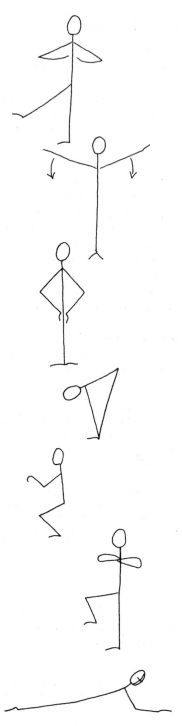

6. *Rooster walk:* Holding the head and chest high, strut forward lifting legs with knees straight and hands at the side of the chest. Wiggle elbows to imitate flapping wings.

7. *Birds:* Stand on tiptoe and wave the arms slowly up and down. As the "wings" move faster, run on tiptoe to imitate birds flying. As the flapping slows, the birds slowly come in for a landing.

8. *Robin hop:* Stand with feet together, hands on hips. Hop forward on both toes simultaneously, keeping feet together, pretending to be a robin.

9. *Ostrich:* Bend forward at the waist and grasp the ankles. Walk forward keeping the knees as stiff as possible, stretching the neck in and out.

10. *Kangaroo:* Stand with the feet together, elbows bent with hands dangling limply in front of the body. Bend the knees deeply and jump forward from both feet simultaneously.

11. *Prancing horses:* Stand with the arms folded across the chest. Hold the head upward and back. Prance, lifting feet high and pointing toes.

12. *Seal or walrus walk:* Lying face down on the floor, push chest off the floor with the arms and keep the knees straight. Walk forward with the arms and allow the legs to drag behind.

13. *Frog jump:* Assume a squat position with hands placed well in front of the body on the floor between the legs; travel forward by leaping forward to hands, bringing legs up to squat position. Replace hands well in front of the body after each jump.

14. *Pollywog crawl:* Face down on hands and feet in the push-up position with back and legs straight, walk forward with the hands, advancing with short steps by hunching hips and bending ankles. This stunt requires a great deal of arm and shoulder strength.

15. *Crab walk:* From a sitting position, reach backward and place hands flat on the floor. Lift the hips off the floor and walk in the direction of the feet (on hands and feet), keeping head and body in a straight line.

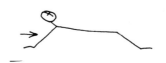

16. *Lobster walk:* Same position as Crab walk. Walk in the direction of the hands, keeping head and body in a straight line.

17. *Measuring worm:* Support the body on hands and feet with the legs extended backwards in a push-up position. Keep hands in place and knees stiff while walking on toes in short steps until feet are near hands. Keeping feet in place, walk forward with hands using short steps until starting position is reached.

18. *Bounding ball:* Bend the knees so that the hands and feet touch the floor, hands at shoulder width and feet 24 inches apart; back and legs are kept in a vertical line. Travel forward by means of a series of short upward springs of the hands and feet simultaneously.

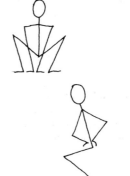

19. *Duck waddle:* Assume a bent knee position with hands on hips. Walk forward while retaining this position. Do not bend knees to a full squat; the knees should not form an angle greater than 90 degrees.

20. *Chicken walk:* Assume a squat position with the feet together and knees apart. Grasp ankles with left hand on left ankle, right hand on right ankle. Walk forward in this position.

21. *Gorilla walk:* Bend knees slightly, bend trunk forward with the arms hanging down until the back of the hands touch the ground. Walk forward in this position.

22. *Toe grasp walk:* Bend the knees slightly, and bend the trunk forward. Grasp the toes with the left hand holding the left toe, right hand on right toe. Walk forward in this position.

23. *Ankle grasp walk:* Bend trunk at hips and grasp left ankle with left hand and right ankle with right hand. Walk forward, keeping knees as stiff as possible.

24. *Crouch run:* Lean forward at the waist until the trunk is parallel with the ground. Run forward at a jogging pace in this position.

25. *Toe touch walk:* Walk forward, bending trunk forward and touching one hand to the toe of the opposite foot with each step. Raise trunk to an erect position between steps.

26. *Heel touch walk:* Walk forward with fairly long steps, reach back and touch the heel of the rear foot after each step (right hand touches right heel and left hand touches left heel).

27. *Knee touch walk:* Walk forward bending knees and touching the knee of rear leg to the ground on each step. Knees are bent and straightened on each step.

28. *Walk on toes:* Walk forward on tiptoe taking very little steps. Raise hands above head as tall as possible.

29. *Giant step walk:* Walk forward, making each step as long as possible.

30. *Fast walk:* Walk forward as fast as possible without running. Swing arms vigorously.

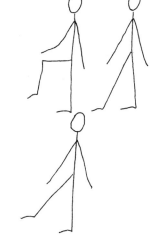

31. *Knee raise walk:* Walk forward, raising the bent knee of the advancing leg as high as possible. Lengthen each step by extending the leg forward after the knee has been brought up.

32. *Goose step walk:* Walk forward without bending the knees, lifting the advancing foot hip high. The steps should be of normal length. Swing the arm opposite to the lifted leg.

33. *Knee raise run:* Run forward, raising the knee of the advancing leg as high as possible with each step.

34. *Hop on left foot:* Travel forward by hopping on the left foot. The direction of travel may be altered to provide varying levels of body control. Repeat on the right foot.

35. *Hobble hop on left foot:* Bend the right leg and grasp right foot with the left hand behind the buttocks. Hop forward on the left foot, then backward and in different directions. Repeat, bending the left leg and hopping on the right foot.

36. *Broad jumps:* Travel forward by a series of jumps, leaving both feet simultaneously.

37. *Step-hop:* Travel forward in a series of steps and hops. Step with left foot, hop on left foot; step with right foot, hop on right foot.

38. *Human rocker:* Lie face down, reach back and grasp both ankles. Keeping the knees spread apart, rock the body back and forth.

39. *Log roll:* Lie across one end of a tumbling mat with arms extended overhead. Roll over and over evenly in one direction by twisting the shoulder and hips. Keep the trunk as stiff as possible.

40. *Forward roll:* Using a gymnastic mat, squat and place the hands on the mat about shoulder width apart. Place chin on chest and lean forward, pushing with the feet and bending the arms. Allow the back of the shoulders to touch the mat first as the roll is executed and continue rolling over on the back. When the shoulders touch the mat, take the hands from the mat and grasp the ankles, pulling the body into a tight ball. Roll forward in this small ball position and then straighten to a standing position.

41. *Backward roll:* Start from a squatting position with the hands on the mat and the knees between the arms. Lean slightly forward and then backward into the roll. Push with the hands, sit down and start to roll onto the back. Place the hands above the shoulders with the fingers pointed back and the palms up. Keep the chin on the chest throughout the roll. Roll over the top of the head and on to the hands, keeping the knees tucked in close to the chest. Push with the hands and continue the roll to the feet. Finish in a squat position.

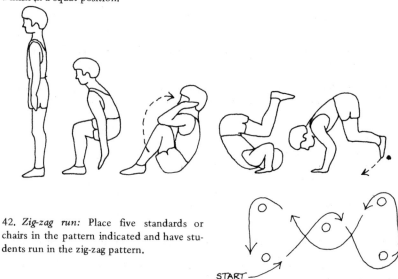

42. *Zig-zag run:* Place five standards or chairs in the pattern indicated and have students run in the zig-zag pattern.

START

43. *Figure eight run:* Paint or tape the indicated pattern on the floor. Have students follow the lines in a figure eight fashion.

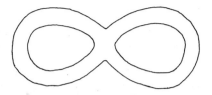

44. *Straddle jumps:* With feet and legs together, jump into alternate black squares painted on the floor as indicated. Vary with half-turns or jumps from square to square. Each block is 18 inches square.

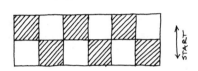

45. *Dodging run:* Place a series of standards or chairs as indicated. Have the student weave in and out of the pattern while running. A ball may be dribbled or kicked through the course for variety.

46. *Obstacle course:* A well-designed obstacle course provides varied physical activity that is individualized, progressive, and self-testing in nature. Whether purchased or built by parents and teachers, ideal obstacle course equipment should be adaptable for children at varying levels of proficiency and require a large variety of motor responses. Directions for the construction of obstacle course units are given in Chapter 12.

SENSORIMOTOR PERCEPTION

Perceptual-motor or sensorimotor skills are highly developed activities requiring the interaction of the sensory, muscular, and central nervous systems. Often these activities are so taken for granted that one fails to realize the complexity and learning involved in their development. The perception of spatial patterns and relationships; the estimation of speed, distance, and depth; the identification of patterns of sound; and the sensory information supplied by the muscle sense organs are all components of many complex processes.

The sensorimotor skills most frequently required in our daily activities include eye-hand and eye-foot coordination; fine muscular control for activities such as grasping, releasing, and manipulating various objects; the timing required to catch or dodge moving objects; and the ability to aim at targets after rapidly estimating required elements such as weight and depth. Because many senses and fine muscular controls are needed, these skills are developed by assigning the student tasks that include the component parts of these judgments and skills. These activites are not usually found in a program for normal children and many physical educators exclude them from the realm of physical education. However, the special needs of the retarded child require that activities such as the following be an integral part of their education.

Visual Tracking

1. *Pendulum:* Hang a ball on a cord from the ceiling; have the child follow its path with his eyes, and point at it with his finger.

2. *Marsden ball:* This is a ball suspended on a cord from a pole. Swing it to and fro and have the child watch it. Have the child lie on his back; swing the ball in large circles and ask the child to watch it until it stops.

3. *Marble track:* Have the child look at a marble as it goes from the top of the track to the bottom. The child may point at the marble with his finger if necessary. (This apparatus is described in Chapter 12.)

4. *Identification:* Have the child look at different items or places in the room. Sit in front of the child and show him familiar objects requiring him to name them and to change his visual fixation. Hand objects to the child from various angles and positions so that he must look at and reach for them.

Eye-Hand and Eye-Foot Coordination

1. *Throwing and catching:* Have the child throw and catch various sizes of balls. Begin with large balls that are rolled rather than thrown, if the child finds this difficult.

2. *Kicking and trapping:* Have the child kick and stop balls of varying sizes with his foot. Begin with large, stationary balls, if the child finds this difficult.

3. *Miscellaneous activities:* The following activities are effective in improving eye coordination: pick-up sticks, block building, picking up marbles, clay modeling, tying knots, stringing beads, tracing forms and lines, target games, nail or peg pounding, peg board activities, stepping on footprints the teacher has placed on the floor.

Visual Perception

1. *Stencil or template activity:* Using a stencil or template, the child traces around the form on the chalk board, colors the shape within the stencil form or colors the traced shape without the aid of the stencil.

2. *Block designs:* The teacher uses a series of blocks to make a design which the student is instructed to copy.

3. *Peg board patterns:* The teacher makes designs or combinations of colors that the student copies.

4. *Chalk board games and activities:* Effective activities include: drawing lines to connect dots placed on the board by the teacher; using chalk in both hands; drawing circles with both hands (circles may go out from midpoint, in from midpoint, both hands may travel clockwise, both hands go counter-clockwise); drawing horizontal lines with both hands simultaneously; drawing vertical lines with both hands simultaneously; and drawing lines to specific points on a clock pattern as instructed.

5. *Other activities:* Matching objects, naming objects, naming forms, assembling pictures, and finding missing parts of old pictures (i.e., cut the fenders off a picture of a car).

Discrimination

1. *Matching sounds:* Have several objects that rattle (i.e., cardboard in a small tin container); the student matches those that make the same sound. The student may also be requested to rank them from loudest to softest.

2. *Matching textures:* Place several objects in a paper bag or cardboard box (i.e., scraps of cloth, sandpaper, sponges). The student is required to match the texture or sort them from roughest to smoothest.

3. *Weight discrimination:* The student ranks a series of objects of different weights from heaviest to lightest.

4. *Categories:* The student sorts a variety of objects into categories; such as, objects that write, objects used to eat, objects that are soft.

5. *Imitation:* The teacher performs certain movements (raising one arm) or rhythms which the children attempt to imitate.

6. *Games:* The following games, described in Chapter 10, are effective in teaching discrimination: Simon Says, Follow the Leader, Crow and Crane, Birds Fly, Statues, and Angels in the Snow.

SPEED OF MOVEMENT

The layman usually thinks of speed of movement as the amount of time required to respond to a stimulus as well as the amount of time required to make the desired movement. The scientist, however, would define the time that passes from the presentation of a stimulus until the movement is completed as performance time or completion time. Performance time actually comprises both reaction time, or the rapidity with which one can react to a stimulus once it appears (the time needed to start a movement), and movement time, or the time required to make a movement from its start to its finish. Various authors (Oxendine, 1968; Singer, 1968) have summarized research that indicates there is no relationship between reaction time and movement time. Thus, this component of perceptual-motor behavior relates to the speed with which a series of gross, rapid movements can be made, not the speed of reaction (Cumbee, 1954; Cumbee, et al., 1957; Fleishman, 1954 and 1957; Fleishman and Hempel, 1954).

Unlike the other components of perceptual-motor performance which may be improved by practice of specific activities, speed of movement does not appear to be improved by instruction in specific movements. Henry (1960) has indicated that speed of movement is specific to the task being performed and is therefore faster in well-learned tasks than in new, unfamiliar situations. Fleishman and Hemple (1954) also indicated that speed of movement becomes more important as training progresses and is consequently related to learning.

Summarizing extensive research, Fitts and Posner (1967) described the characteristics of individuals and tasks that influence performance. Among the factors influencing the speed of movement are the amount of information presented, the ability to recognize the important cues or stimuli, the ability to focus attention on the task, the ability to find and identify the important pattern from an array of stimuli, and the variety and repetition of the required responses. Each of these factors is dependent upon learning; once the important cues or patterns are learned, it takes less time to recognize them. Practice reduces the time required to find and identify a learned pattern located among other patterns; movements become quicker and more specific as extraneous actions are reduced with practice. Thus, the time required to initiate and complete a movement is reduced and performance appears more automatic as experience increases. This pattern of improvement holds true with visual, auditory, kinesthetic and other forms of stimulation.

The teacher must recognize that when success depends upon rapid movements the child must receive extensive training and practice on the task. The rapidity of the child's performance will increase as the task becomes better learned. It is also possible that activities selected in a systematic fashion to expose the child to a wide range of movements, such as are presented in this book, may facilitate the child's initial acquisition of new skills. An understanding of the role and nature of speed of movement in performance should help the teacher guide the students in their performance.

SUMMARY

The four components of perceptual-motor behavior are considered to be balance, coordination, sensorimotor perception, and speed of movement. Balance, the development of a sense of equilibrium in both dynamic and static postures, is basic to all activities; it supplies both postural control and a reference system for future actions and judgments. Coordination is the ability to combine many muscular movements into a smooth, well-integrated pattern of movement. It requires quick and accurate change of direction as well as proper timing and rhythm. Sensorimotor perceptions are highly complex processes that provide the fine control needed for grasping, releasing, catching, throwing and similar activities. Speed of movement refers to the speed with which a series of gross, rapid movements can be made.

Although it is impossible to separate these components during the performance of any one activity, it is important to understand their relative contributions to the child's achievement. The teacher of the mentally retarded can utilize many of the suggested activities to develop the various components of perceptual-motor performance.

REFERENCES

Bass, R. I.: An analysis of the components of tests of semicircular canal function and of static and dynamic balance. *Res. Quart.* 10:33–52, 1939.

Cumbee, F. Z.: A factorial analysis of motor co-ordination. *Res. Quart.* 25:412–428, 1954.

Cumbee, F. Z., Meyer, M., and Peterson, G.: Factorial analysis of motor co-ordination variables for third and fourth grade girls. *Res. Quart.* 28:100–108, 1957.

Drowatzky, J. N., and Zuccato, F. C.: Interrelationships between selected measures of static and dynamic balance. *Res. Quart.* 38:509–510, 1967.

Fitts, P. M., and Posner, M. I.: *Human Performance.* Belmont, Calif.: Wadsworth, 1967.

Fleishman, E. A.: Dimensional analysis of psychomotor abilities. *J. Exp. Psychol.* 48:438–453, 1954.

Fleishman, E. A.: A comparative study of aptitude patterns in unskilled and skilled psychomotor performances. *J. Appl. Psychol.* 41:263–272, 1957.

Fleishman, E. A., and Hempel, W. E., Jr.: Changes in factor structure of a complex psychomotor test as a function of practice. *Psychometrika* 19:239–252, 1954.

Fleishman, E. A., and Hempel, W. E., Jr.: Factorial analysis of complex psychomotor performance and related skills. *J. Appl. Psychol.* 40:96–104, 1956.

Guilford, J. P.: A system of the psychomotor abilities. *Amer. J. Psychol.* 71:164–174, 1958.

Henry, F. M., and Rogers, D. E.: Increased response latency for complicated movements and a "memory drum" theory of neuromotor reaction. *Res. Quart.* 31:448–458, 1960.

Kephart, N. C.: Perceptual-motor aspects of learning disabilities. *Exceptional Child.* 31:201–206, 1964.

Oxendine, J. B.: *Psychology of Motor Learning.* New York: Appleton-Century-Crofts, 1968.

Piaget, J., and Inhelder, B.: *The Child's Conception of Space.* New York: W. W. Norton, 1967.

Seashore, H. G.: The development of a beam-walking test and its use in measuring development of balance in children. *Res. Quart.* 18:246–259, 1947.

Singer, R. N.: *Motor Learning and Human Performance.* New York: Macmillan, 1968.

Smith, K. U., and Smith, W. M.: *Perception and Motion: An Analysis of Space-structured Behavior.* Philadelphia: W. B. Saunders, 1962.

Travis, R. C.: An experimental analysis of dynamic and static equilibrium. *J. Exp. Psychol.* 35:216–234, 1945.

CHAPTER 9

Sports Skills

The skills that are used in various sports and recreational situations are specialized extensions of the basic movement skills discussed in earlier chapters. Because sports activities are extensions of basic skills, sports instruction should not be attempted until the basic movements are adequately developed. Note that the basic skills used in basketball, football, soccer, softball, and volleyball may also be used in a variety of low organized games and relays.

BASKETBALL

Success in basketball requires some ability in the fundamental skills of throwing and catching in addition to the specialized techniques involved in shooting and dribbling. The variety of situations that call for the use of basketball skills makes it possible for the teacher to plan practice sessions in interesting and changing situations.

Catching. Success in catching the ball depends upon both the thrower and the catcher. It is easiest for the catcher to control the ball when it is thrown to him at waist or chest height. The ball should be caught near the body with the fingers spread and pointing either up or down, the elbows bent and the wrists relaxed to give with the ball. The basketball should strike the palm of the hand first and the fingers should quickly tighten on the ball to hold it. As contact is made with the ball, the elbows, wrists, and arms must give with the ball to dissipate the force and bring the ball into position for the next movement.

Passing. A number of different passing styles are used in basketball. Which pass to select depends on the type of game taught and the size and ability of the players. Two of the most widely used and easily controlled passes are the two-hand chest pass and the two-hand bounce pass.

The two-hand chest pass begins with the ball held in front of and close to the chest. The ball is held by the finger tips with one hand placed on either side of it. To execute a pass, the arms are quickly extended and there is a decided wrist snap. The hands and fingers follow through in the direction the ball is thrown. A step with either foot should be taken to assist in giving the ball momentum.

Figure 9–1. The two-hand chest pass.

The bounce pass is made in the same way except that the ball is directed toward the floor so that it bounces before being caught by a teammate. This pass is of great value in passing to a teammate when a player is closely guarded. With either pass, the player should attempt to throw the ball so his teammate can catch the ball at either waist or chest height.

Shooting. Successful shooting depends upon the player taking proper aim from a good body position, and placing the ball on a good trajectory. Proper aim is achieved by sighting at the point on the rim that is nearest to the shooter. Good body position results from the player having proper balance with his feet either spread apart or placed one slightly in front of the other. Distance and direction are determined by the force and direction of the arm extension and wrist snap; a high arc is more desirable than a low trajectory. The following shots are among those most commonly taught:

The Two-Hand Set Shot. The ball should be held by both hands with the fingers spread along the sides and upper half of the ball, the thumbs along the side, the feet spread slightly and the weight slightly forward. To execute the shot, the ball is raised to eye level, and after a circular motion by the arms and wrists, the ball is released toward the basket by an extension of the arms. After the ball has left the hands, the arms should follow through to their full extension above the head.

Figure 9—2. The two-hand set shot.

The One-Hand Push Shot. The following description is for a right handed player; the arms would be reversed for a left handed person. The ball is held by both hands, with the left hand on the bottom of the ball and the right hand on the back of the ball just in front of the face. The right foot is one step in front of the left and the weight is slightly forward. To execute the shot, the knees are bent slightly to lower the body, the ball is elevated with the left hand, and the right hand moves down slightly so that it now rests more on the bottom of the ball. From this position the legs and right arm are extended toward the basket and a follow through is continued after the ball leaves the hand.

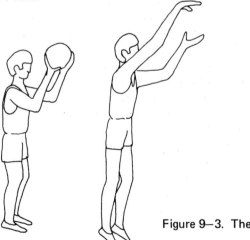

Figure 9—3. The one-hand push shot.

The Lay-up Shot. The lay-up shot should be executed with the right hand from the right side of the court and the left hand from the left side. The player springs from the floor using the foot opposite the hand which will be used to make the shot. The ball should be released at the peak of the jump, with the guide hand under the ball and the shooting hand behind the ball. The shooting arm is extended and the ball is shot against the backboard above the basket.

Figure 9—4. The lay-up shot.

Dribbling. Once the dribbling skill has been mastered, the player should be able to use either hand equally well. The arm and hand not in use should be poised loosely at the side of the ball so the ball can be caught or transferred as necessary. The ball is controlled by the wrist and fingers; the fingers control the direction of the bounce and the wrist supplies the force. The ball is thus pushed forward and downward as the player moves down the court. If the player is dribbling by himself his body may be erect, but a crouched position is used when the player is guarded. The head and eyes should be kept up at all times.

FOOTBALL

Touch football is a widely played game that retains most of the fundamentals of regular football. The rules for touch football are not as standardized as those of tackle football, but the elements described here apply equally well to both games.

Blocking. The purpose of offensive blocking is either to remove an opponent from the path of the ball carrier or to prevent an opponent from reaching the ball carrier. In touch football a player is not permitted to leave his feet during a block so he must maintain his balance while retaining a position between the defensive man and the ball carrier. The block is executed by placing the shoulder in contact with the opponent midway between his knees and hips. The hands should be held at the chest with elbows spread. Once contact is made the offensive man must keep shouldering or pushing the defensive man until the ball carrier has gone by the area.

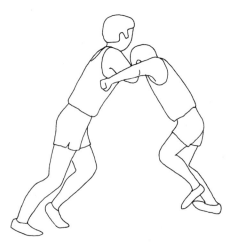

Figure 9—5. Offensive blocking.

Passing. The pass in football is a form of the overhand throwing pattern. Because of its shape, there are two basic ways of holding the ball: (1) gripping it with the fingers or (2) allowing the ball to lie in the palm of the hand. The grip pass should be used if the player's hand is large enough to permit gripping. To grip the ball a player should place his fingers over the lacing and slightly behind the middle of the ball. It should be gripped firmly. The left hand should help control the ball while the right hand grips it. The right foot should be planted on the ground and the body weight shifted back on that foot before throwing the ball. The arm is cocked back behind the ear on short passes and is brought back further on longer passes. The throwing motion is the same as for the basic overarm throw with the transfer of body weight and follow-through being important elements of the successful pass. The palm pass is made in the same manner except that the ball is not gripped by the throwing hand.

Figure 9—6. Holding the ball to pass.

Catching. The receiver is generally in motion and may be running directly away from the passer, diagonally away, or at right angles in front of the passer. The pass receiver must not take his eyes off the ball once it has been thrown if he is to judge its speed and direction correctly. The pass should be caught with the hands and immediately brought down to the body and tucked in the regular carrying position under the armpit. Successful catching requires that the fingers are well spread and the hands give slightly upon contact with the ball.

Centering the Ball. The center usually places the ball in play in touch football with a spiral pass. To center the ball from a lineman's stance the right hand is placed on the side and under the front half of the ball, while the left hand is on the back half of the ball, the thumb on top and the fingers on the side. To pass the ball between the legs, the arms are brought quickly backward and the wrists snap to supply the necessary spiraling motion to the ball. The center must look at the player to whom he is passing the ball.

Figure 9—7. Centering the ball.

Punting. The punter receives the ball in his outstretched hands from the center. He places the ball in his hands the way he wants to hold it before placing it on his foot and then takes a half step with his right foot, followed by a full step with the left. As the kicker takes these steps, the ball is carried in front of him. As the left foot is placed on the ground, the ball is released and kicked with the instep of the right foot. The ball should not be dropped or thrown, but should be kept under control by the right hand until just before the foot makes contact with the ball. The flat side of the ball should be placed on the instep of the foot.

Figure 9—8. The football punt.

SOCCER

Successful soccer players master the technique of controlling the ball with their feet by keeping the ball reasonably close to their bodies while advancing it. The ball should also be kept close to the ground rather than in the air. The fundamental kicking skills are the inside-of-foot kick, the outside-of-foot kick, and dribbling. Trapping refers to the methods used to stop and control a moving ball and heading may be used to advance a ball when it is above chin height.

Kicking with Inside-of-Foot. The kicking leg is brought back with the knee slightly bent and toe extended. The leg is then brought forward with the toe close to the ground and turned outward. When the inside of the foot contacts the ball, the knee is straightened. The non-kicking foot should be planted near the ball. Direction of the ball may be controlled by changing the direction that the toe is pointing and distance may be increased by kicking the ball with the toe or the instep. The farther the leg follows through, the higher the ball will go.

Figure 9—9. Kicking with the inside-of-foot.

Kicking with Outisde-of-Foot. This kick is performed in the same manner as above except that the ball is contacted with the outside-of-foot. This kick tends to send the ball to the right while the inside-of-foot kick may be used to send the ball to the left. The angle to the right will depend upon the extent to which the foot is turned inward; the more the foot is turned inward, the more nearly forward the ball will be kicked.

Dribbling. Dribbling is used by a player to advance the ball while still retaining possession of it. The ball is pushed along the ground by kicking it gently with either the inside or the outside of the foot. The ball is usually dribbled using first one foot and then the other to keep it moving in a fairly straight line just ahead of the player.

Trapping. Moving balls may be stopped with either the body or feet. Several effective methods of trapping are used by advanced players. A rolling, bouncing, or slightly air-borne ball may be trapped by placing a foot on top of the ball just as it strikes the ground or immediately after. If the ball is bouncing high, it may be met with either the calf or the thigh. The leg contacting the ball in this manner must remain limp and give with the ball so that it will drop immediately in front of the player. Balls that are above the waist are usually trapped by the stomach or chest. The body moves back as it contacts the ball to reduce the ball's momentum and direct it to the ground near the feet of the player.

Heading. When a ball is air-borne above chin height, heading is used to stop or control it. The ball should be contacted with the top of the forehead at the hairline. the neck and spine are held rigid and the feet should be off the ground to minimize the shock. The ball will rebound from the head, but greater distance may be gained by using the neck muscles and driving the ball away. The eyes must follow the flight of the ball until contact between the head and ball is made. A player should never attempt to head a ball that is below chest height.

SOFTBALL

Softball is a team sport involving several fundamental movement patterns. The game may be modified in a number of ways to either increase or decrease the difficulty of the fundamental skills involved. The fundamental softball skills of throwing, catching, and batting may also be used in a variety of low organized games and recreational activities.

Throwing. The throwing activities used in softball, the single underarm and single overarm throws, have been described in Chapter 7. The underarm throw must be used in pitching but the overarm throw is used in most other cases because it yields more accuracy. The players must be taught to make the throws quickly, accurately, and to the correct base. The two basic softball games played today use either fast pitch or slow pitch rules. Under fast pitch rules no restrictions are placed upon the speed or type of pitches used and the ability of the pitcher determines to a large extent the success of the team. If the slow pitch rules are used, the ball must travel from the pitcher to the batter in an arc with a height of 12 inches or more. This modification enables more balls to be hit and allows the other fielders a greater role in the team's success.

Catching. The two types of moving balls that must be handled by every player are those in the air that have not hit the ground and those which are rolling or bounding along at various rates of speed. In catching a ball above waist level, the player should hold his hands with thumbs together, fingers up, and palms away from the body. To catch a ball below waist level the hands should be held with the little fingers together and the palms away from the body. In both cases the fingers should be cupped and the hands and wrists are relaxed to give with the ball. When fielding ground balls, the player should stand with his feet comfortably spread and the body weight evenly distributed on the balls of both feet. The hands should be held low with the glove near or on the ground. The body should be bent from the hips with the knees only slightly bent. All balls should be played in front of the body if possible to allow the player to block any missed balls with his body. Whenever catching a ball it is important that the fielders should watch the ball all the way into their hands.

Batting. Most hitters should grip the bat with their hands close together and the lower hand approximately 3 inches from the end of the bat. The lower hand should always be the one on the side facing the pitcher; that is, the left hand for the right-handed batters and the right hand for the left-handed batters. The bat should be gripped with the trademark placed on top. This marking indicates the way the grain of the wood runs and the bat may break if the ball is struck firmly on that spot. The feet should be comfortably spread and the body weight evenly distributed on the balls of the feet for a good batting stance. The hitter should stand close enough to the place to be able to reach the far side of the plate with the end of the bat. The bat is cocked back about as far as the ear. The swing should be executed in a horizontal plane with the transfer of body weight as the front foot strides toward the pitcher. The bat should follow through after meeting the ball while the feet remain on the ground. The rear foot should make the initial step toward first base since the weight has been shifted to the front foot during the swing.

VOLLEYBALL

The most effective method of teaching children to play volleyball is to first develop the fundamental skills used in the game. Once these skills are developed, lead-up games such as Newcomb and modified versions of volleyball may be used to refine performances and teach the rules of the game. This is especially necessary with volleyball because few, if any, other sports use the same techniques. Three basic principles should be used to start the instruction: (1) beginners should use two hands exclusively; (2) the ball should be held by the fingers, not the palm of the hand; and (3) beginning students should keep the hands near the level of the face. Only the fundamentals of handling and serving the ball will be presented here; the more advanced techniques of spiking and blocking are described in the references listed at the end of the chapter.

Handling the Ball. Two basic types of passing, one for a low ball and the other for a high ball, are used. Regardless of the position of the ball, it should always be played with both hands if at all possible. Using only one hand for these passes is considered poor form and makes control very difficult.

Passing the High Ball. Most balls are received above the waist, permitting the player to make a chest pass. To receive the ball, the feet should be fairly well spread and the body in a crouched position. The hands should be held about the level of the face in a cupped position with the fingers spread so that the thumbs and finger tips alone touch the ball. With the hands in this position the thumbs should be together and the palms pointing forward and upward in the direction the ball will travel. Once the ball is contacted by the finger tips, the entire body aids in hitting the ball. The legs straighten from their flexed position and the arms also extend to direct the ball upward. The player must face in the direction the ball is to travel as it should always be directed straight in front of him.

Figure 9–10. Passing the high ball.

Passing the Low Ball. Any ball that is played at waist height or lower is considered a low ball. To play a low ball, the feet should be spread, the body crouched, arms flexed at the elbows, and the hands and fingers cupped. The hands in this position should be held with the little fingers together and the thumbs pointing outward. The ball is played by straightening the knees and swinging the arms through a lifting motion in the direction in which it is desired that the ball move. The actual contact with the ball is made on the fingers. Although this technique differs somewhat from that used in international rules, retarded children have more success with this method. Again, the player must face in the direction the ball is to travel.

Figure 9—11. Position of the hands to control the low ball (above) contrasted with the hands for the high ball (below).

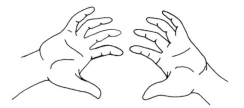

Underhand Serve. The simplest way to begin a play in volleyball is with the underhand serve. To make an underhand serve, the players stand facing the net with the ball resting on the left hand. The left foot is in front of the right and the body is in a stooped position. The ball is held by the right side of the body and is struck off the left hand by the right hand with an open palm, a clenched fist, or the back side of the closed hand. The open palm is the easiest method for a beginner to learn and is the easiest to control.

Figure 9—12. The underhand serve.

SUMMARY

The fundamental skills used in basketball, football, soccer, softball, and volleyball are specialized developments of the fundamental movement patterns described in Chapter 7. It is important that the student adequately develop the fundamental movement patterns before attempting to learn specific sports skills. The retarded child may require instruction in the elements of catching, throwing and kicking before he is able to participate in sports. For the more advanced skills of various games the teacher should consult one of the following references.

REFERENCES

Basketball

Bee, Clair, and Norton, Ken: *Basketball Fundamentals and Techniques,* 2nd ed. New York: Ronald Press Company, 1959.
Bunn, John W.: *Basketball Techniques and Team Play.* Englewood Cliffs, N.J.: Prentice-Hall, 1964.
Hobson, Howard A.: *Basketball Illustrated.* New York: Ronald Press Co., 1948.

Football

Grombach, J. U.: *Touch Football.* New York: A. S. Barnes and Co., 1936.
Holgate, James: *Fundamental Football.* New York: Ronald Press Co., 1958.

Soccer

DiClements, Frank F.: *Soccer Illustrated.* New York: A. S. Barnes & Co., 1955.
Hankinson, J. T., and Chadder, A. H.: *Soccer for Schools.* London: George Allen and Unwin Ltd., 1951.
Waters, Earl C., Eiler, John R., and Florio, A. E.: *Soccer.* rev. ed. Annapolis: U.S. Naval Institute, 1950.

Softball

Coombs, J. W.: *Baseball: Individual Play and Team Strategy,* 3rd ed. Englewood Cliffs, N.J.: Prentice-Hall, 1951.
Noren, Arthur T.: *Softball: With Official Rules,* 3rd ed. New York: Ronald Press Co., 1966.
Vogel, O. H.: *Ins and Outs of Baseball.* St. Louis: C. V. Mosby Company, 1952.

Volleyball

Leveaga, Robert E.: *Volleyball,* 2nd ed. New York: The Ronald Press Co., 1960.
Welch, J. Edmund (Ed.): *How to Play and Teach Volleyball.* New York: Association Press, 1960.

General

Blake, O. William: *Lead-up Games to Team Sports.* Englewood Cliffs, N.J.: Prentice-Hall, 1964.

CHAPTER 10

Low Organized Games
and Lead-Up Activities

The basic motor skills described in preceding chapters are of fundamental importance in helping the retarded child to achieve his maximum potential. His effective functional or adaptive behavior requires that he be able to respond to differing situations with a series of appropriate motor patterns.

In games the teacher of the mentally retarded has the opportunity to combine many of the specific skills developed through instruction in their component parts. Basic motor skills or patterns can be used in properly selected games to elicit the desired adaptive responses and help the child in this way to achieve increasing levels of independence. Games also enable the teacher to present a controlled mix of social and motor situations.

Through proper selection or modification of games, the teacher can, to some extent, tailor the situation for the children. According to Thompson (1962), games play a vital role in developing social maturity and moving the exceptional child toward the behavior norms of our culture. With increasing chronological and mental age, the child engages in more associative and co-operative activities and decreases the amount of time spent in solitary play and passive observation.

Farina *et al.* (1959) summarize the principles to be considered in the selection of games and activities for children as follows:

1. The games must be based on a knowledge of the child's developmental characteristics, including growth patterns, muscular development, social maturity, and game interests.

2. Safety of the children is a prime consideration in game selection. Equipment must be in good repair and the teacher must know how to use it. Clothing, special equipment such as braces or hearing aids, the playing area and the like must be considered when selecting activities for the handicapped child.

110

3. The teacher should understand the techniques of adapting games to the amount of space, the number of children and type of play involved.

4. The socio-psychological characteristics of the children are important factors in game selection. Children from different socio-economic backgrounds have different abilities and needs; frustrating game situations may bring out a variety of adjustment mechanisms with which the teacher must cope.

This chapter describes activities that are organized into tag and dodging games, discrimination or alertness games, throwing and catching games, and lead-up games, a variety of activities that encompasses a wide range of abilities, situations and interests. The level of difficulty of each game may be changed by modifying the rules or changing the equipment used, for example, a larger ball, bigger target or lower basketball goal. Whether the child achieves his goal in the game depends upon the teacher's selection and teaching skill; it must be emphasized, however, that games are not an end, but rather a means to the end.

TAG GAMES

TAG

Objectives: Running, dodging

Area: Playground or large activity room

Equipment: None

One student is selected to be chaser. He pursues the others, trying to tag any one of them. They are free to run wherever they wish. When a runner is tagged, he immediately becomes chaser. No "touch-backs" are allowed until the old chaser has had enough time to get away from the new chaser.

BOUNDARY TAG

Objectives: Running, dodging

Area: Playground, gymnasium, or activity room

Equipment: None

Boundary Tag is Tag played within boundary lines, and with the provision that any runner who touches the ground out of bounds is considered tagged. (Any runner who crosses the line is out.) The playing court should be fairly small, a volleyball court or half of a basketball court being the desired size in most cases. No immediate "touch-backs" are allowed.

WOOD TAG

Objectives: Running, dodging

Area: Playground or activity room

Equipment: Wood or other items used as safe bases

The rules are the same as Tag, except that a runner cannot be tagged while he is touching any piece of wood. The teacher can rule that growing plants are not considered wood or designate other items as safe bases.

SKUNK TAG

Objectives: Running, dodging, bending and identifing body parts
Area: Playground or activity room
Equipment: None

A runner cannot be tagged while he holds one foot in either hand and his nose in the other. Instead of the foot, he may be required to hold an ankle or other body part in one hand. A restricted area is recommended for this tag game.

RUN, RABBIT, RUN

Objectives: Running, dodging
Area: Playground or activity room
Equipment: None

The hunter stands facing the runners, who are in line a short distance from him. The hunter points to an object some distance away—a tree, post, mat, wall, or the like, and then calls "Run, rabbit, run." All the runners flee toward the designated object and are safe from tagging when they reach it. The hunter pursues them and tries to tag the rabbits before they reach the place of safety. The person tagged may become a second hunter, or if only one hunter is desired he becomes the new hunter. If more than one hunter is used, the last rabbit to be caught is the winner.

POM-POM-PULLAWAY

Objectives: Running, dodging, alertness development
Area: Playground or activity room
Equipment: None

This game requires a court with two parallel lines about 60 feet apart and side lines of about 50 feet apart. One student is chosen as first chaser and he takes his position in the middle of the field. All the other players are runners, who stand behind one of the two parallel goal lines. The chaser calls in a loud voice, "Pom-pom-pullaway, come away or I'll pull you away." At the completion of the call, all players run for the opposite goal line and as they do, the chaser tries to tag one of them three times. The runner who is tagged three times, becomes the second chaser. Then the two chasers stand in the middle, issue the call, and try to tag runners as they run back to the original goal line. The call is given only by the original chaser. The surviving runners continue to change goals, while all who have been tagged act as chasers. This continues until the last runner has been tagged. He is the winner of the game. Any number of runners may be tagged on one chase. When a new game is started, the usual custom is that the first player tagged in the preceding game is the first chaser in the new game. Sometimes the right to be the first chaser is considered an honor, and is given to the man who was last tagged. The game may be varied with the runners divided equally between the two lines, each man running from his respective line to the other; or the chasers may be required to tag only once.

LAME FOX

Objectives: Running, dodging, hopping, alertness development

Area: Playground or activity room

Equipment: None

The fox stands in the center of a 10-foot circle, with the runners scattered outside the circle at random. The runners tantalize the fox by coming into the circle, taunting him with such expressions as "lame fox, lame fox, can't catch anybody." As he desires, the fox pursues the runners. While the fox is in the circle he may run, but outside of the circle he must hop. There is no safety base and the fox continues the pursuit until he tags a runner, although he may at any time return to his circle and make a fresh start. Boundaries, such as a basketball court, may be used if desired.

MIDNIGHT

Objectives: Running, dodging, alertness development

Area: Playground or activity room

Equipment: None

The chaser stands within a small circle and the others approach as close to him as they dare asking "What time is it?" The chaser gives any answer he desires, such as "One o'clock" or "Three o'clock". The runners continue to question until the answer "Midnight" is given. Then all runners flee to a safe base some distance away, with the chaser in pursuit. All persons tagged join the chaser in his circle and the game proceeds as before. The last person caught becomes the chaser in the next game. Only the original chaser replies with the time.

KICKOFF TAG

Objectives: Running, dodging, catching, carrying, blocking

Area: Playground

Equipment: Football, soccerball, or playground ball

The teams line up for a kickoff as in a regular football game, except that the field need not be of standard size. One team makes a kickoff and the other returns it, as in a football game, until the runner is touched. As soon as he is touched by an opponent he is stopped and the players prepare for the next chase. The teams now trade places and the kickoff is made by the team that received the first kick. The teams continue to alternate kicking and receiving for an agreed number of plays.

Each team scores points according to the distance that the ball is returned, and the team with the larger score at the end of the game is the winner. For ease in scoring, the field should be divided into five-yard zones and the zones numbered from the goal line. The score on each run-back is the number of the zone to which the ball is returned. For example, the man with the ball scores four points if he is tagged in the fourth zone.

STEAL THE BACON

Objectives: Running, dodging, grasping, alertness development

Area: Playground, activity room

Equipment: Item to serve as "bacon" such as eraser, bean bag, Indian club, or handerchief

The item serving as the "bacon" is placed midway between two parallel goal lines where two equal teams of players line up to await their turn. A starting signal is given and a player from each team, designated by name or number, runs to the "bacon" where each of them has a choice: (1) he can score a point by picking up the item and returning with it to his own goal line without being tagged by the other man, or (2) he can score a point by allowing the other man to pick up the item and then tagging this man before he returns to his goal line. The team accumulating the most points wins the game.

HEADS AND TAILS

Objectives: Running, dodging, alertness development

Area: Playground or activity room

Equipment: Coin

Two goal lines are marked about 50 feet apart. The players are divided into two easily distinguishable teams. A neutral leader tosses a coin and calls the side that comes up. If he calls "heads," all members of the heads team run for their goal while the other team attempts to tag them. All players tagged join the other team. If he calls "tails," the tails team runs for its base while the heads team attempts to tag them. The team that tags all members of the other team is the winner.

TRADES

Objectives: Running, dodging, development of basic body movements and alertness

Area: Playground or activity room

Equipment: None

Two equal teams face each other from parallel goal lines several feet apart. Team B, selected as chaser, remains on its line and Team A marches up close to it. After a short dialog, Team A acts out the motions suggestive of a trade, occupation, or activity. A correct guess by Team B is the signal for the chase and the acting Team A rushes back to its goal with Team B pursuing it and tagging as many of its members as possible. The game is repeated with the roles of the two teams reversed and the numbers tagged are compared. The following example is typical of the dialog commonly used. Team A is the acting and Team B is the chasing team.

Team A: "Here we come."

Team B: "Where are you from?"

Team A: "New York." (Or "New Orleans.")

Team B: "What's your trade?"

Team A: "Lemonade."

Team B: "How's it made?" (Or "Show us some if you're not afraid.")

At this point the acting and guessing of the trade begin. If necessary, Team A gives the initials of the trade, or other hints.

In this game, as in many others, it is sometimes specified that a man tagged in one chase becomes a member of the enemy team for the next chase.

WOLF

Objectives: Running, dodging, alertness development

Area: Playground

Equipment: None

One man, chosen to be the original chaser, hides as the other players gather around a goal with eyes closed and count for a designated time. When the count is completed, the runners go in search of the chaser. When any runner finds the chaser he calls, "Wolf!" and this word is the signal for the chase. The chaser then pursues the runners who flee to the safe base. A man tagged by the chaser is the chaser the next time. The game may be played with more than one chaser, hiding in the same or different places. For variety, when a runner is tagged on his way to the goal he has the right to tag another runner, and this person still a third runner, and so on, the last runner tagged being the first chaser of the next game.

FOX AND GEESE

Objectives: Running, dodging

Area: Playground (or other appropriately marked areas)

Equipment: None

This game is traditionally played in the snow and is the best known snow game. Paths are marked by trampling the snow, forming a large wheel with a hub, spokes, and a double rim as show below. The size of the wheel varies with the number and age of the players but should have a diameter of at least 30 feet, with the inner rim located about 6 feet from the outer one. All players run at will, but they may not leave the paths. The intersections of the spokes and the outer rim are safety spots and a runner who stands on one of these is immune to tagging. The number of safety spots should be one less than the number of runners. The teacher may rule that a runner is forced from his safety spot by a new arrival. With the exceptions noted, the game is the same as Tag.

Figure 10—1. Pattern for Fox and Geese.

DODGING GAMES

BALL TAG

Objectives: Running, dodging, throwing

Area: Playground or activity room

Equipment: Partially deflated ball, such as a volleyball or soft playground ball

This game is the same as Tag except that the chaser carries a ball while running and may tag a runner either by touching him with the ball held in his hand, or by throwing the ball and hitting him with it. All players run at random, and any hit counts, whether direct or on the roll or bounce. When the ball is thrown and missed, retrieving it may cause an undesirable slowing of the game. This delay can be eliminated by playing the game in a relatively small room where the ball can rebound from the walls. When this is impossible the game can be played with two throwers working together. The throwers pass the ball from one to the other as often as they wish before making a throw. A runner who is hit trades places with the one who hits him.

WALL DODGEBALL

Objectives: Dodging, throwing, alertness development

Area: Side of building or activity room wall

Equipment: Partially deflated ball, such as a volleyball or soft playground ball

All players, except one, line up against a wall. The remaining player stands behind a line several feet from the wall. He throws a ball at the players near the wall, trying to hit them. If one of the players is hit, he may either trade places with the thrower or join the thrower in attempting to hit the remaining players. If the latter alternative is chosen, the last player to leave the wall is the winner.

ONE-MAN DODGEBALL

Objectives: Dodging, throwing, alertness development

Area: Playground or activity room

Equipment: Partially deflated ball, such as a volleyball or soft playground ball

One man runs at will within a circle formed by the others, who stand facing the center. The circle players have a ball that they pass among themselves and throw at the center man who attempts to dodge the ball. A circle man who hits the center man trades places with him.

CIRCLE DODGEBALL

Objectives: Throwing, dodging, alertness development

Area: Playground or activity room

Equipment: Partially deflated ball, such as a volleyball or soft playground ball

Players are in two teams, one inside and the other outside a circle about 30 feet in diameter. The men of the outer team have a ball that they pass about at will and throw at the center team whenever they wish. A man on the throwing team may enter the circle to retrieve the ball, but he must never throw it except when outside the circle. When a man is hit by the ball, he immediately leaves the circle and the game. The game continues until all the inner players are eliminated. The two teams then reverse positions and the game is played again. Time may be kept and the winner is the team that eliminates its opponents in the shorter time, or each team may be in the circle for a prescribed time and the winner determined by comparing the number of survivors at the expiration of the time. Two balls may be used to speed up the game.

BOMBARDMENT

Objectives: Dodging, throwing, alertness development

Area: Activity room or playground

Equipment: Partially deflated ball, such as a volleyball or soft playground ball

The game is played on a rectangular field with two equal courts, each about 30 feet square. Players are in two teams, one in each of the courts. One team has a ball that it throws at the other. Only direct hits are valid and only one hit can count from each throw. The ball must not be caught, since catching it would cause the catcher to be hit. Any man hit with the ball immediately withdraws from the game. Whether or not the first throw is successful, the opponents of the throwing team retrieve the ball and throw it back at the other team. Thus, the ball is thrown back and forth until all members of one team have been eliminated. In order to limit retrieving time as much as possible, the game should be played in a room small enough to consider the whole area the playing field. If this is not possible, eliminated players should be stationed out of bounds to recover the ball. The game may be varied by providing that a man who catches the ball cleanly is not considered hit, while anyone who muffs the ball is considered hit. Two or three balls may be used to speed up the game.

FOUR-COURT DODGEBALL

Objectives: Dodging, throwing, alertness development

Area: Activity room or playground

Equipment: Partially deflated ball, such as volleyball or soft playground ball

A rectangular area is divided into four courts as indicated in Figure 10-2. Players are in two teams, initially occupying areas one and two. Each team has a ball with which it tries to hit the opponents. If no one is hit directly

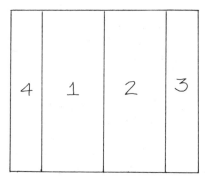

Figure 10-2. Layout for Four-Court Dodgeball.

(without a bounce) the opponents of the throwing team retrieve the ball and throw it back. If a member of the team in court one is hit, he goes to court three; he retrieves any ball coming into his court and either throws it at his opponents or passes to a team member in the other court. Members of the team in court two go to court four when hit and the team with all players eliminated from the center court is the losing team. For variety, more than one ball may be used.

CUMULATIVE DODGEBALL

Objectives: Throwing, dodging, alertness development

Area: Activity room or playground

Equipment: Partially deflated ball, such as volleyball or soft playground ball

A circle about 20 feet in diameter is drawn on the ground. One man stands outside the circle, all others move at will inside. The outside man has a ball that he throws at the others; if he misses, he must recover the ball himself and continues to throw until he hits one of the men in the circle. The man who is hit goes outside the circle and becomes a second thrower. The two throwers now cooperate in hitting the others and may pass the ball from one to the other as often as they wish. As soon as other men are hit, they join the throwers, so that the number of throwers increases as the number of center men decreases. The game continues until only the winner is left in the circle. Since the first thrower is likely to have some difficulty in making a hit, it may be well to start with two throwers. This game can be played in an enclosed area to reduce retrieval time.

SPUD

Objectives: Throwing, catching, alertness development

Area: Activity room or playground

Equipment: Partially deflated ball, such as a volleyball or soft playground ball

One man has a ball and the other players gather informally around him. The man with the ball tosses it into the air calling the name of another player as he does so. The man whose name is called rushes for the ball, catches or recovers it as quickly as possible. Then he calls "Halt," and the others who have fled must stop in their tracks. The ball is then thrown at any of the other players who are allowed to move only one of their feet in dodging. If a man is hit by the throw he recovers the ball, calls "Halt," and throws it at any other players, the players meanwhile having fled from him. This is repeated as long as the throws are successful. When a throw is unsuccessful and does not hit anyone, play starts as at the beginning of the game, the thrower who has failed to hit a runner being the one to toss the ball and call the name of the next thrower.

This game is sometimes played with a penalty, a point scored against a man for being hit and a penalty received for acquiring a prescribed number of such points. A point may be scored against a man for being hit, for missing a throw, or for either.

THROWING AND CATCHING GAMES

CIRCLE PASSBALL

Objectives: Throwing, catching, alertness development

Area: Playground, activity room

Equipment: Ball

All players stand in a single circle at intervals of 3 feet or more, the interval depending on the kind of ball used and the ability of the players. The ball is thrown from one man to another, entirely at random and as quickly as possible. When a man makes a bad throw or fails to catch a good one, he is eliminated and the game continues until only one person is left. A throw is considered good if the catcher is able to touch it with both hands. The game can be played without elimination, using negative scores and a penalty. A player who is eliminated may be required to sit on the ground in his place or to turn around to face the rear.

TEACHER AND CLASS

Objectives: Catching, throwing

Area: Playground, activity room

Equipment: Ball

One player is designated as the teacher and stands facing the others, who stand in an arc of a circle. The teacher throws the ball to the others in turn, starting with the player on his right. Each player catches the ball and throws it back to the teacher. If a player misses the ball he goes to the left of the line. If the teacher misses a throw he goes to the left of the line and the player on the right becomes a teacher. If the teacher does not miss while the ball goes twice around, he returns to line at the right of the players who have missed, and the player at the right takes his place.

STEP-BY-STEP

Objectives: Catching, throwing

Area: Playground, activity room, hall or other area having a flight of stairs

Equipment: Ball

All players but one sit side by side on the bottom of a flight of steps. The odd player stands some distance in front of and facing the others. He throws a ball to the others in turn and they throw it back to him, exactly as in Teacher and Class. If the odd man misses a throw, he is replaced by the thrower. There is no penalty for a miss by the other players, but a player who does not miss moves up to the next step. The first one to reach the top step is the winner. All players must be given an equal number of chances. If two or more reach the top at the same time, the others are eliminated and the winners play off the tie, starting at the bottom again.

TAGBALL

Objectives: Throwing, catching
Area: Playground, activity room
Equipment: Ball

One player stands in a circle formed by all the others. The circle men have a ball that they throw from one to another at random, trying to prevent its being touched by the center man. The center man tries to touch the ball; when he does so he indicates which man he thinks made the error that permitted him to touch the ball and he and this man then trade places. His chances vary with the kind of ball and the ability of the players; for this reason the game should be adjusted so that any center man can succeed in touching the ball within a reasonable time. Probably the best way is to restrict the method of throwing or to limit the men to whom a man may throw. For example, it may be ruled that the ball must bounce on the floor. A ball that is missed and touches the floor as a result should be considered as touched by the center man. Two men may be in the center at the same time to provide variation.

CIRCLE MISSBALL

Objectives: Throwing, catching, alertness development
Area: Playground, activity room
Equipment: Two balls

One man stands in the center of a circle formed by the other players. The center man has one ball and one of the circle men has another. At a signal, the circle man throws his ball to the center man and the center man throws his ball to the player on the circle who stands on the left of the first thrower. Throwing is continued rapidly and without hesitation, going around the circle to the left; a circle man who receives the ball returns it immediately to the center man and the center man always throws his ball to the man at the left of the circle thrower. This continues until the center man fails to catch a throw; when he does so, he trades places with the thrower.

CIRCLE CALL BALL

Objectives: Throwing, catching, alertness development

Area: Playground, activity room

Equipment: Ball

One man stands in the center of a circle formed by the other players and tosses a ball into the air, calling one of the circle players by name or number. The person called tries to catch the ball before it strikes the ground. If he succeeds he is next center man; otherwise the same man repeats. The game may be scored with penalties, each miss counting as a negative point. To make this game easier, the ball may be caught on the first bounce.

KEEPAWAY

Objectives: Throwing, catching, alertness development

Area: Playground, activity room

Equipment: Ball

Players are in two distinguishable teams scattered at random within boundary lines, such as those of a basketball court. The men of one team have a ball that they pass among themselves while the other team tries to get the ball. Touching the ball is not enough, since actual possession is required. If the ball is acquired by the other team, the game continues with the teams changing their roles. The rules of basketball apply except that dribbling is not permitted. There is no scoring in this game.

VARIETY KEEPAWAY

Objectives: Throwing, catching, alertness development

Area: Playground, activity room

Equipment: Ball

Same as Keepaway, except that only a specified method of throwing the ball may be used. The method may be changed frequently at the direction of the leader.

VOLLEY KEEPAWAY

Objectives: Striking, development of eye-hand coordination and alertness

Area: Activity room, playground

Equipment: Volleyball

Similar to Keepaway, except that it is played with a volleyball that is batted from one player to another rather than caught and thrown.

BEANBAG PASSING

Objectives: Throwing, catching, alertness development

Area: Playground, activity room

Equipment: Beanbag for every other player, or half the group, with one beanbag a distinctive color

Players form a single circle, all facing inward. The space between the players depends on the skill of the group in tossing and catching. Every second child is given a beanbag, with one player, the leader, having the colored one. At a signal the players holding beanbags turn to the right and toss their bags to their right-hand neighbor. These players immediately turn to the left to receive the beanbag which will be coming to them. The game ends when the leader receives the distinctive colored beanbag with which he started play. The game may be repeated as often as desired. As players become proficient, additional beanbags are introduced and the distance between players is increased.

BEANBAG BOXES

Objectives: Throwing, development of eye-hand coordination

Area: Playground, activity room

Equipment: (1) Five beanbags or small balls; (2) three cardboard or wooden boxes of different sizes fastened one inside the other with a space of approximately six inches between the walls of the boxes. The center box should be approximately six inches wide. The boxes may remain flat on the floor or they may be tilted.

A throwing line is drawn not less than 8 feet from the front edge of the largest box. Players stand with both feet back of the throwing line when playing. The first player steps to the throwing line and throws his five balls or beanbags, one at a time, trying to land them completely within a box area. Beanbags which remain on the edge of a box wall or partition do not score. When the player has thrown, the bags are collected and the second player tries.

A beanbag falling in the center of the smallest box scores 3 points; a beanbag falling into the middle space scores 2 points; one falling into the outside space between the third and second box scores 1 point. At the beginning of the game the players decide whether they will play for 10, 15, 20, or a smaller number of points, depending on the skill of the players. The player who first earns the total number of points agreed upon is the winner.

INFORMAL HORSESHOE-PITCHING

Objective: Throwing skills

Area: Playground

Equipment: Horseshoes and stakes

Inexperienced players may use an adaptation of the official rules for Horseshoe Pitching. The box may be dispensed with and the stakes driven into any level piece of ground. The distance may be estimated rather than measured accurately. The scoring may vary, with a game ending at 21 points instead of the official 50. Sometimes a ringer counts five, and quite commonly a "leaner" counts three or two. Another variation provides that if a ringer tops one or more other ringers, then the top one receives the score of all put together. These variations may be replaced by the official rules as the game is mastered. The use of hard rubber horseshoes is recommended.

QUOITS

Objectives: Throwing, development of eye-hand coordination

Area: Playground

Equipment: Quoits, stakes

Horseshoe Pitching rules or traditional quoit rules may be used. The quoit is shaped like a doughnut except that one surface is flat and the other convex; the inside diameter is 4 inches, the outside diameter 9 inches, and the rim is 2½ inches wide. The pins project from the ground only 1 inch and are about 50 feet apart. (The distance should be reduced considerably for retarded children.) A ringer counts three points and a hobber or leaner, two points. If two or more ringers are thrown, the top one receives the scores of all of them, as in Informal Horseshoe-Pitching. A game ends at 21 points.

BOMBARDMENT

Objectives: Throwing, catching, alertness development

Area: Activity room

Equipment: Balls, Indian clubs

A rectangular court about 50 feet long is divided in half by a line across the middle. The game should be played in a room with walls at each end, so that the balls can rebound from the walls. The end lines are 3 to 5 feet from the walls. A row of Indian clubs is placed on each end line. One club for each player may be satisfactory, but the number and arrangement of the clubs should be determined by experiment. Players are divided into two equal teams, and each team is restricted to one half of the court. The game is played with several balls, which may be softballs, basketballs, or any other balls that are not hard enough to be dangerous. At least six balls should be used, and it is better to use more, since it is difficult to have too many. Half of the balls are given to each team. At a signal from the teacher, players begin to throw the balls, trying to knock down the clubs that the opponents guard. Any player who can get a ball may throw it at the clubs, or he may pass it to a teammate, the only restriction being that each man must remain in his own half of the court. A defender may block a ball by catching it or by stopping it with any part of his body. When a club is down it stays down, but may be slid to one side to get it out of the way. At the end of the predetermined time, the team with the larger number of clubs standing is the winner.

CENTER STRIDE BALL

Objectives: Kicking, trapping, striking, throwing, catching

Area: Playground, activity room

Equipment: Volleyball, basketball, soccer ball, or partially deflated utility ball

All the players but one form a circle facing inward. One player enters the center and is given the ball. The circle players take a natural stride position with their feet touching the feet of their neighbors. The center player tries to throw or roll the ball so that it will pass outside the circle either between the feet of a player or between the bodies of two players but below their shoulders. The circle players keep their feet stationary and stop the ball by using their hands. Circle players may throw or bat the ball to keep it away from the center man, and protect their own space with their hands.

If the ball passes to the outside between a player's feet, that player secures the ball and changes places with the center player. If the ball passes to the outside between the bodies of two players, the person on whose right side the ball left the circle secures it and changes positions with the center player. If the circle player is able to pass the ball outside by putting it between the feet of one of his two neighbors, the neighbor secures the ball and becomes the center player.

DISCRIMINATION (ALERTNESS) GAMES

CROWS AND CRANES

Objectives: Running, dodging, alertness development

Area: Playground, activity room

Equipment: None

The players are divided into two equal teams facing each other about 2 or 3 feet apart. Each team has a safety line 15 or 20 feet behind them. One team is designated crows and the other cranes. The teacher calls either "crows" or "cranes," always prolonging the first part of the word, as "Crrrows." The team called must attempt to reach its base line without being tagged by the other team which attempts to catch them. Any person caught must join the chasing team and the first team to catch all members of the other is the winner.

RUN, SHEEP, RUN

Objectives: Running, alertness development

Area: Playground or activity area with hiding places

Equipment: None

The players are divided into two equal teams, each with a captain. All members of one team close their eyes at the goal and count, while all of the other team members, except the captain, run and hide. After the count, the counting team goes in search of the hiders, the captain of the hiders being free to accompany the searchers or to go wherever he pleases. When one of the searchers spies any one of the hiders he notifies his captain, who calls "Run, sheep, run!" at which signal all members of both teams race for the goal. The first man to reach the goal wins for his team. The game may be continued with the roles of the two teams reversed or with the losing team designated as hiders. If the captain of the hiding team considers it wise, he may give the call, "Run, sheep, run" at any time, and then the chase is on as before.

The winner of a race may also be determined by the last man to reach the goal, rather than the first. In other words, the winner is the first team to get all of its men to the goal.

FOLLOW THE LEADER

Objectives: Development of locomotor patterns and alertness

Area: Playground, activity room

Equipment: Any desired to provide obstacles, stunts or other activities

A leader is selected. The other children line up behind the leader in single file formation. The leader sets patterns for the children to perform. He may jump forward, climb apparatus, crawl under a bench, run, skip, walk with long strides, perform stunts, or, twisting and turning, lead the group where he desires. The others follow and try to perform accurately the patterns set by the leader. Children who fail to perform the stipulated activity go to the rear of the file.

ANGELS-IN-THE-SNOW

Objectives: Development of body awareness and alertness

Area: Activity room

Equipment: None

The child lies on his back on the floor with his arms at his side and his feet together. The child is then given a series of movements to perform by the teacher. The commands may be given verbally or by pointing to the body part, or a combination of the two. The commands might be as follows: (1) move both arms over your head; (2) move your feet apart; (3) move just this arm (point to right arm), now back; (4) move just this leg (point to left or right leg), now back; (5) move this arm and this leg (point to one arm and leg in varying combinations), now back.

The game may also be played outdoors in the snow. The child lies down in the snow, moves his arms and legs, and then gets up and looks at the patterns created as a result of his movements.

STATUES

Objectives: Development of locomotor patterns and alertness

Area: Playground, playroom, gymnasium, hallway, auditorium

Equipment: None

All the players but one line up along and behind the starting line that is parallel to and 30 feet or more from the finish line. The odd player or leader stands beyond the finish line with his back to the starting line and gives the signals. Without turning to look at the advancing players, he calls "Come on!" The players advance in any way they wish—walking, running, hopping, skipping, turning, or jumping. The leader signals in some way that he is going to turn—by shouting, clapping his hands three times, waving his hands high in the air, jumping into the air, or by counting loudly to ten. When he finishes the signal and turns, the advancing players must stop suddenly and "freeze" into position. If the leader sees any player or players in motion he sends them back to the starting line to begin again. The leader again turns his back and gives the signal. Play goes on until at least half the advancing players succeed in crossing the finish line. The first player to cross the finish line is the leader for the new game.

STOP AND START

Objectives: Development of locomotor patterns and alertness

Area: Playground, activity room

Equipment: Whistle

Children stand about the room watching the leader. As the leader points, the children begin to move in that direction. When the whistle is blown, they stop and turn to watch the leader for the next direction. Children who fail to stop immediately or who fail to follow directions form a second group of players on the opposite side of the leader. The object of the game is to see who will be the last player in the original group. It is possible to vary the game by telling the children to fly, hop, skip, run, crawl, or jump as they move.

HORNS

Objective: Alertness development

Area: Playground, activity room, classroom

Equipment: None

All players sit facing a leader, each with both forefingers extended downward and touching the table. A leader calls "dog's horns up," or "cow's horns up," or ". . . . . horns up," naming some animal. If the animal named is one that has horns, all must lift their forefingers and point them upward, but if the animal does not have horns, all must remain motionless. The leader tries to confuse the players by raising his fingers at an inappropriate time. The leader may also call "All horns up," and they all must raise their fingers. The player who makes an error or is too slow in making a correct response trades places with the leader.

ELEPHANTS FLY

Objective: Alertness development

Area: Playground, activity room, gymnasium, auditorium, hallway, classroom

Equipment: None

Players stand either in circle formation or in line formation with a leader standing in front of the middle of the line. The leader calls "Butterflies fly!" and all the children wave their arms in flying motion. He may then say, "Crows fly!" and the action is repeated. If he should say, "Elephants fly!", any child who waves his arms must exchange places with the leader, since elephants do not fly, even if the leader stated so.

DUCKS FLY

Objectives: Development of alertness, locomotor activities, basic movements

Area: Playground, activity room

Equipment: None

The players line up before a leader who must be able to observe them closely. The leader calls the name of an animal or object, followed by a verb indicating some kind of activity. If the activity named is one performed by the animal or object, then all the children try to imitate the activity; if the called activity is not appropriate, then all must remain motionless. The leader tries to confuse the others by making motions at the wrong time. A player who makes an error may trade places with the leader, be eliminated, or have a point scored against him.

I SAY STOOP

Objective: Alertness development

Area: Playground, activity room, classroom

Equipment: None

A leader stands before the group and gives commands of "I say stoop" or "I say stand" in quick succession. At the former command each player must do a full squat and immediately return to a stand; at the latter command he must remain motionless. The leader, as he gives the commands, tries to mislead the players by performing actions which are sometimes different from the commands. That is, he may command "I say stand" and then may stoop and rise; or he may command "I say stoop" and remain standing, in the hope that some player will imitate him rather than follow his command. Anyone who makes a mistake is eliminated.

SIMON SAYS

Objectives: Development of locomotor patterns and alertness

Area: Playground, activity room

Equipment: None

The leader stands in front of a group, who may stand or sit, although standing is preferred. The leader gives commands such as "jump," "sit," or "turn around." If he precedes the command with, "Simon says," then all players must obey. If he omits "Simon says," the command is to be ignored. If a player fails to obey a command preceded by "Simon says," or if he obeys one not preceded by the phrase, he is eliminated.

DO THIS, DO THAT

Objectives: Development of locomotor patterns and alertness

Area: Playground, activity room, classroom

Equipment: None

A leader stands before the other players, performing various movements or exercises. As he does each movement he calls either "do this" or "do that." If the movement is accompanied by the command "do this" all must imitate the movement, but if it is accompanied by the command "do that" all must remain motionless. The first child to make an error trades places with the leader.

CONTRARY CHILDREN

Objective: Alertness development

Area: Playground, activity room, classroom

Equipment: None

A leader stands before the other players and gives commands to which each player must respond by doing the opposite. For example, to the command "Right foot forward" the player extends the left foot forward. To the command "One step forward" he takes one step backward, and so on. Sometimes there may be more than one correct response. Anyone who makes an error is eliminated.

SQUIRRELS IN THE TREE

Objective: Alertness development
Area: Playground, activity room
Equipment: None

All players except one stand in groups of four, three forming a tree by placing hands on one another's shoulders, the fourth standing inside as a squirrel. The groups may be scattered at random or may be in a circle. The odd man is a squirrel without a tree. At a signal from the odd man or from a neutral leader, each squirrel must leave his tree and try to get another with the odd man also trying to get a tree. The one who is left without a tree is odd man next time. At frequent intervals, one of the tree men should trade places with the squirrel. Each tree may be formed by only two players instead of three for small groups.

I SPY

Objectives: Running, alertness development
Area: Playground with hiding places
Equipment: None

All players except one run and hide while the odd man covers his eyes and counts to a prescribed number. As soon as the count is completed the odd man goes in search of the hiders. When he sees one he calls. "I spy . . . .," and the two race for home base where the odd man did the counting. The same man then goes in search of other hiders and the game continues until all hiders have run home. The first of the hiders to lose his race with the odd man is the odd man next time. Any man in hiding may run home before being spied if he believes he can make it before the odd man.

The odd man may count by ones or by fives to any designated number while the others hide.

THROW-THE-STICK

Objectives: Running, alertness development
Area: Playground with hiding places
Equipment: A stick

This game is essentially the same as I Spy, with the counting replaced by throwing and retrieving a stick. All the players gather around a tree or other base against which it is possible to lean a short stick. One player is selected as odd man while any other player takes the stick in his hand and throws it as far as he can. All players except the odd man immediately run and hide, as in I Spy, but the odd man must run for the stick, bring it back, and lean it against the goal; then he goes in search of the hiders. From this point on, the game is the same as I Spy, except that any hider who beats the odd man in the race to the goal may pick up the stick and throw it. The odd man must then retrive the stick again before proceeding with his search for hiders.

STOP—GO

Objectives: Development of locomotor patterns and alertness

Area: Playground or activity room with hiding places

Equipment: None

The odd man covers his eyes, counts to ten, and then opens his eyes. As he counts the others move toward but do not need to reach places of hiding. When the odd man opens his eyes the others must either be in hiding or remain motionless. Any player seen moving must return to the goal and make a fresh start. Again the odd man covers his eyes and counts to ten, and the process is repeated until all have hidden, any man seen moving always being required to make a fresh start. When all have reached places of hiding, the odd man seeks them and the game from here on is the same as I Spy. It may be advisable to place a limit on the number of times that the odd man is to count, and any man who has not reached a place of hiding then is considered a loser. If the number of counts is limited, the last one should be longer than the others, say twenty-five instead of ten.

BASKETBALL SKILLS

TWENTY-ONE

Objectives: Lead-up game to basketball; development of eye-hand coordination

Area: Playground or activity room with basketball goals

Equipment: Basketball

Twenty-One is a basketball goal-throwing game for two players. The players stand together on a throwing line at any suitable distance from a basket. The line may be drawn or imagined. One of the men throws the ball at the goal, runs in to recover it, and shoots again from the spot of recovery. He scores two points for a successful long shot and one point for a successful short or follow-up shot. When he has completed his turn he throws the ball to his opponent who takes the same shots. The players take turns throwing first. As soon as either man has scored 21 points the game is over, except that both men must have had the same number of shots; thus, if the first thrower in any inning scores 21 points the second player still takes his turn (provided he has a chance to win or tie). A common difficulty arises when, after the long shot, the ball is received beyond the end line where it may be impossible to shoot at the basket. Sometimes the player is permitted to dribble the ball to a position where he can shoot but it is recommended, instead, that the player lose his shot unless he can make it without violating the basketball rule against traveling with the ball. The following variations in the game are common: (1) To win a game, a man must score exactly 21 points, rather than 21 or more, as in the basic game. If he scores more than 21 his score reverts to zero. (2) The short shot is not taken unless the long one is recovered before it has bounced twice. (3) A successful long shot counts three instead of two. (4) The short shot is not taken, except when the long one is missed. If this variation is used, it is suggested that three points be counted for a long shot. (5) If a player makes both the long and short shot, he continues to shoot, alternating long and short shots, until he misses.

THREE, TWO, AND ONE

Objectives: Lead-up activity to basketball, development of eye-hand coordination and alertness

Area: Playground or activity room with basketball goals

Equipment: Basketball

Same game as Twenty-One except for a variation in the scoring. A long shot counts three and a follow-up shot recovered before the ball strikes the floor counts two. Any other follow-up shot counts one.

SPOT-POINT BASKET SHOOT

Objectives: Lead-up activity to basketball, development of eye-hand coordination

Area: Playground or activity room with basketball goals

Equipment: Basketballs

Several spots are marked on the floor around one basketball goal, and different numbers are assigned to them. The spots may be the same or varying distances from the goal. The players have one shot from each spot, starting from spot number one and shooting from the other spots in order. When a throw is successful, the thrower scores according to the number of the spot, a goal from spot four counting four points, for example.

BASKETBALL GOLF

Objectives: Lead-up game to baskctball, development of eye-hand coordination

Area: Playground or activity room with basketball goals

Equipment: Basketball

Nine spots are marked on the floor at varying distances from a basketball goal. Players throw in turn from spot number one, each man following up his missed shot and continuing to shoot from the spot of recovery until he makes the basket. His score is the number of shots required to make the basket. When all have "holed out" from the first spot, they repeat the same process from the other spots in turn. The player with the lowest score is the winner.

AROUND-THE-WORLD

Objectives: Lead-up activity to basketball, development of eye-hand coordination

Area: Playground or activity room with basketball goals

Equipment: Basketball

Use as many baskets as possible, each with its own throwing line. Players line up in single file behind the first throwing line. The first man shoots at the basket and if he makes a goal he moves to the second throwing line and throws at the second basket; if he succeeds again he moves to the third, and so on until he misses, after which he stands behind the line from which he missed. As soon as the first man has finished his turn, the second man does likewise, and so on until every man has had a turn, each man stopping at the line from which he missed. Then they throw again in the same order, each man resuming from the line where he left off. The required round may consist of one goal in each basket or it may require going around them more than once. The game can also be played with only one basket and several throwing lines, the men moving from one line to another with successful shots.

BOWLING SKILLS

IMPROVISED BOWLING

Objectives: Throwing; development of eye-hand coordination

Area: Activity room

Equipment: Ball, bowling pins or substitutes

Bowling pins or substitutes are set up as in the standard game on any smooth floor, such as that of a gymnasium. Players roll a basketball at these pins, scoring as in bowling. Plastic pins and balls are available at various stores.

SCHOOL BOWLING

Objectives: Lead-up activity for bowling, throwing, development of eye-hand coordination

Area: Bowling surface (hard surface), playground, gymnasium, hallway

Playing surface: Painted pin spots 12 inches apart in a triangle arrangement, as in an official bowling game. The apex is toward the player (pin Number 1). Numbers 2 and 3 are in the second line; 4, 5, and 6 in the third; 7, 8, 9 and 10 in the last. A 3-foot foul line is drawn at least 30 feet from the front pin. The distance from the pins to the foul line depends on the age and skill of the player. See Figure 10—3.

Equipment: (1) Cage constructed of 2- x 2-inch wood and ½-inch wire mesh (Figure 10—4) with a mat over the wire to absorb the force and noise of balls and pins. (2) Ten duckpins. Pins with rubber band or inner tubing around them will be less noisy (Figure 10—4). If discarded pins cannot be obtained from local bowling establishments, homemade pins may be constructed from tapered cylindrical soap or milk containers partly filled with sand (Figure 10—5). (3) Two or more duckpin balls of ladies' weight, or 2-pound 14-inch balls of hard rubber similar in size to a baseball. (Black rubber balls leave black marks on the floor.)

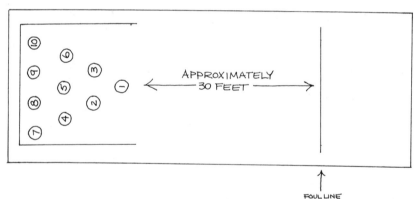

Figure 10—3. Playing surface for School Bowling.

The game can be played by two opponents as singles, by two sets of partners as doubles, or in teams with as many as five members each. Balls are bowled from behind the foul line, two for each player each turn. Players take turns in setting up pins. The object is to roll the ball toward the pins and knock down as many as possible. A game consists of *frames* corresponding to squares on the score sheet into which the score is written. A player bowls twice in each frame unless he makes a strike (knocks down all ten pins with the first ball), in which case he does not bowl a second. Official ten-pin rules are followed.

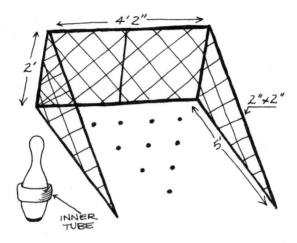

Figure 10—4. Bowling cage and pin with inner tube.

Figure 10—5. Homemade bowling pins.

The score is kept cumulatively on a score sheet marked for ten frames. Each pin knocked down counts 1 point. When one ball knocks down all ten pins, that is called a strike; when ten pins are knocked down with two balls, it is called a spare; when less than ten pins are knocked down, it is called a break. When a strike is made, the bowler get 10 points plus the points made on the next two balls. He therefore does not enter his score until two more balls have been bowled, but instead puts an X in the right-hand corner of the frame. When a spare is made, the bowler adds to the 10 points the number of points he makes on the next ball. He enters a diagonal stroke (half of an X) in the corner of the frame and does not add the total until after the next ball is bowled.

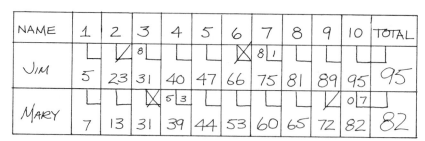

Figure 10—6. Example of bowling score sheet.

Example of scoring: On the first frame Jim made 5 points and on the second he made a spare, so a diagonal line was placed in the corner. On the next ball he scored 8, so 18 points were added to the 5 and placed in the second frame. The total of 31 for the third frame includes the 8 scored in that frame. Nine points were scored in the fourth frame, 7 in the fifth, and a strike was scored in the sixth. An X was marked in the corner and his score for the frame was 19 points, 10 for the strike plus the 9 pins scored on the next two balls. Nine points were scored in the seventh frame, 6 points in the eighth, 8 points in the ninth, and 6 points in the tenth frame, for a total of 95 points for the game.

Mary scored the following points: first, 7; second, 6; third, 18 (10 for the strike plus 8 on the next two balls); fourth, 8; fifth, 5; sixth, 9; seventh, 7; eighth, 5; ninth, 10 (10 points for the spare, no pins were hit with the next ball); and, tenth, 7 for the pins that were struck with the second ball.

If a strike or spare is bowled in the tenth frame, the necessary two or one extra balls, respectively, are bowled. The highest possible score for a game is 300 points.

FOOTBALL SKILLS

FOOTBALL KICK FOR DISTANCE

Objectives: Lead-up to football, kicking

Area: Playground

Equipment: Football

The ball is placed on a kicking tee on a line and each player takes one running kick and one stationary kick. The distances are measured from the point of the base line to the spot where the ball lands. The game is scored by using distance lines, a certain number of points being given for the various distances marked off on the field.

Variation: Instead of using a kicking tee, the players hold the ball and punt it. Scoring is the same as above.

PUNT BACK

Objectives: Lead-up to football, kicking, catching, running

Area: Playground

Equipment: Football

The game may be played on a regulation-size football field, although a somewhat smaller one may be better for handicapped children. Goal posts are not used. Players are in two teams, each team scattered in one half of the field. One team has a football, and one man from this team takes the ball and punts it toward the opponents from a line marked in his half of the field. The line should be located so that a good kick will carry the ball to the opposing team just as far from the middle of the field as is the kicking line. The opposing team tries to catch the ball on the fly. If they succeed they advance the ball three steps and kick it. If the ball is not caught, they kick from the spot where the ball is recovered. In any case, the ball is not necessarily kicked by the man who recovers it, but is always kicked by the players in order, each one taking his proper turn.

The ball is kicked back and forth, each team trying to kick the ball toward the opponent's goal, until one team wins a point by kicking the ball so that it strikes the ground or is caught behind the opponent's goal line. Since one team is almost sure to have some advantage in the location of the first kicking line, a game should never be decided by a single point; after the first point is scored, the teams should change goals and play again. Two variations may be used:

1. Same rules as Punt Back, except that the ball is thrown, instead of being kicked. Any kind of ball may be used, but a softball or football is suggested.

2. Same as Punt Back, except that each player has the option of punting, drop-kicking, or throwing the ball. The teams score by sending the ball over the goal line, according to the method used: drop kick, three points; forward pass, two points; punt, one point.

PUNT AND CATCH

Objectives: Lead-up to football, kicking, catching

Area: Playground

Equipment: Football

The students are divided into two teams and stand along their respective goal lines. The goal lines should be 30 to 60 feet apart, depending upon the skill of the players. The team members number off and take turns attempting to punt the ball over the opponent's goal line. Any member of the opposing team may try to catch the ball. If the ball is caught on the fly, there is no score. If the ball touches the ground before it is stopped, the kicking team gets one point. If the punted ball does not go over the goal line and a member of the opponent's team catches it on the fly, one point goes to the receiver's team. The punting alternates from team to team until each player has had a turn. The team with the most points is the winner. If too many balls fall short of the goal, shorten the distance between lines; lengthen the distance if most players are able to punt well beyond the goal line.

SOCCER SKILLS

SOCCER RELAY

Objectives: Lead-up activity for soccer, kicking, dribbling

Area: Playground or activity room with three 20-foot lines parallel to each other: 12 feet between the first and second; 23 feet between the second and the third

Equipment: For each team a soccer ball, stuffed ball casing, or large utility ball

Teams are organized in file formation, no more than six players on a team, standing behind the first line. The leader of each team holds a ball. At a signal, each leader runs to and across the farthest line, turns, and runs back to the center line, from which point he rolls the ball along the ground to the waiting player. He must not make the return trip until he has touched both feet across the far line. Each team member follows the same procedure until all in one team have finished. When the team leader is back in starting position with the ball in his hands, that team wins.

CIRCLE KICK BALL

Objectives: Lead-up game for soccer, kicking, trapping

Area: Playground, activity room

Equipment: Soccer ball

The players form a circle with hands joined. The ball is placed in front of one of the players to start the game and is then kicked back and forth inside the circle in effort to send it outside the circle under the clasped hands of two players. The two players who permit the ball to pass under their hands are retired and leave the game. If the ball passes outside between the legs of a player, that player is retired. If the ball is kicked outside above the clasped hands of the circle players, the kicker who sent it out is retired.

When not kicking, players try to prevent the ball from passing outside the circle. They may use any part of their bodies to do this with the exception of their hands, which must remain clasped with the hands of their neighbors. The game is continued until three players remain in the circle. They are the winners of the game. Points against players may be used rather than elimination.

Variation: A line is drawn on the ground, separating the players into two teams, A and B. No players are eliminated in this game. One half the circle area is A's territory, the other half, B's. The teams play in stationary positions as they try to kick the ball through. When team formation is used, 2 points are scored for kicking the ball outside the circle according to the rules. Three points are deducted if a player kicks the ball outside the circle over the arms and heads of the circle players. The first team to make 10 points wins.

MASS SOCCER

Objectives: Lead-up activity for soccer, kicking, trapping

Area: Playground or activity room

Equipment: Balls (may be partially deflated).

With mass soccer, teams considerably larger than in the standard game, often 25 or more, can play. It is necessary to eliminate the off-side rule and to simplify other rules. The game is usually played with two balls, but there is no reason why three or four balls could not be used. One goal tender is needed for each ball. The game may be played with a goal wider than the standard one.

INDOOR SOCCER

Objectives: Lead-up game to soccer, development of eye-foot coordination

Area: Playground or activity room

Equipment: Partially inflated soccer ball

This game requires a ball which is soft and less lively than the standard one. A partially inflated soccer ball is usually used, but any other ball that is soft enough will serve the purpose. The goal is improvised, from high-jump standards for example, and the game is played with modified rules.

PIN SOCCER

Objectives: Lead-up game to soccer, development of eye-foot coordination

Area: Playground or activity room

Equipment: Partially inflated soccer ball

This is a special form of simplified indoor soccer. The goal is an Indian club standing in the center of a 6-foot circle, and a point is scored when the club is knocked down. Modified soccer rules are used as desired.

LINE SOCCER

Objectives: Lead-up activity to soccer, kicking, trapping

Area: Playground, activity room

Equipment: Soccer ball or partially inflated playground ball

This game is played without goal posts in a small rectangular field or in an activity room. Each team forms a line with its players along their goal line. At a given signal, two or three designated players from each team go to the center of the field and attempt to kick the ball through the legs or between the players of the opposite team and across the goal line. The ball must go through the line of players below their shoulders. A point is scored when the ball crosses the goal line passing between the players who attempt to prevent this by kicking the ball or blocking it with their bodies. The players in the center of the field use modified rules of soccer. After a point is scored, or after a designated period of time, the players in the center of the court rotate with the other members of their respective teams.

SOFTBALL SKILLS

KICKBALL

Objectives: Lead-up activity to softball, catching, throwing, kicking, running
Area: Playground or activity room with a softball diamond with bases 30 feet apart; pitcher's line 15 to 20 feet from home plate
Equipment: (1) Four bases made of wood, linoleum, or sacks filled with sand or sawdust; (2) utility ball or soccer ball

Players are divided into two teams. One team stands behind home plate and each member takes his turn as the kicker. The other team goes to the field, with a pitcher, catcher and fielders. After three members of the kicking team have been put out, the kicking team goes to the field and the fielding team becomes the kickers. Players rotate positions on the field so that each child has a chance to pitch and catch.

The game is played according to softball rules, with the following exceptions: (1) The pitcher rolls the ball to the waiting kicker, who attempts to kick the ball into the field and then run to first, second, third, and home bases before being tagged or thrown out by the other team. He may not steal or play off bases while the ball is in the pitcher's hands preparatory to a roll. (2) A base runner is out if "tagged out" or "thrown out" before reaching first, second, third, or home plate. He is tagged out if the ball is in the hands of the baseman or fielder when he tags the base runner. Runner is thrown out if the base is touched before the runner reaches it, either (a) by the ball while in the hands of the baseman of fielder, or (b) by some part of the body of the baseman or fielder while holding the ball.

Each successful run to home plate scores 1 point. The team that has more points at the end of a designated number of innings wins. Kickball can be played without pitching as follows: (1) the "batter" stands at home plate with a volleyball and makes a legal volleyball serve with it; (2) the batter stands at home plate with the ball in his hand and throws it; or (3) the batter stands at home plate with a soccer ball and punts it. Otherwise softball rules are used.

ONE OLD CAT

Objectives: Lead-up activity for softball, catching, throwing, striking, running

Area: Playground

Equipment: Softball, bat, and base

This game requires a diamond for the determination of fair and foul balls, but the only bases actually used are home and first. There are no teams; each man plays for himself: there is only one batter at any given time, the rest of the players being fielders. Ideally the game requires ten men, one batter and nine fielders, but it may be played with fewer than nine fielders. First base, the only one used except home, must be placed closer to home than the official distance. Pitching and batting are the same as in baseball or softball, but the base running is different. When the batter has a fair ball, he must run to first base and back to home. There is no such thing as being safe at first. Consequently, the usual play of the fielders is at home and not at first base. If the batter makes a run, he immediately bats again and continues to do so until he is out. When the batter is out, he takes the last place in the field and each fielder moves up one position according to a definite system. The catcher always becomes batter and the pitcher becomes catcher. The other moves are not well standardized, but the most common is for the outfielders to move to the left and the infielders to the right. In this system the right fielder is in last position and the move is from this position to center field, left field, third base, shortstop, second base, first base, pitcher, catcher, batter.

LONG BASE

Objectives: Lead-up game to softball, catching, throwing, running, striking

Area: Playground

Equipment: Soft ball, bat

A home plate and a long base, a rectangle about 5 by 8 feet, about 60 feet from home are required. A pitcher's plate is marked between home and long base, either at the standard softball distance of 46 feet or at any other distance that seems suitable. The game is played with standard softball bats and soft balls. Pitching is the same as in softball, but the batter must run on any ball that touches his bat no matter how slight or in what direction it goes. He must run to long base and may stop there if he arrives safely. He is out only if a fly ball is caught or if he is hit with a thrown ball. A man on base is not forced off by a subsequent hit but may remain there as long as he wishes, except that if he does not get home in time for his next turn at bat, he is out. This rule allows several men to be on the base at one time and at a favorable

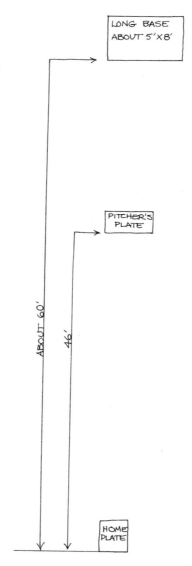

Figure 10—7. Playing area for Long Base.

opportunity they all may rush for home. A base runner need not run in a straight line but may deviate from it as much as he wishes, although it is well to establish boundaries, either marked or imaginary, beyond which a runner may not go.

LONG BALL

Objectives: Lead-up game to softball, running, throwing, catching, striking

Area: Playground, or activity room with a home plate and a pitcher's box 30 to 40 feet away from it; first and third base lines (used only to determine fair or foul balls); long base, placed to the right of home plate and 65 feet away from it. The base may be represented by a 3- x 3-foot wood or linoleum square, or pole, tree, jumping standard, sack of sand, or chair. An extended 40-foot safety line is drawn across the playing field touching the rear of home plate.

Equipment: One 12-inch softball; two softball bats in various sizes.

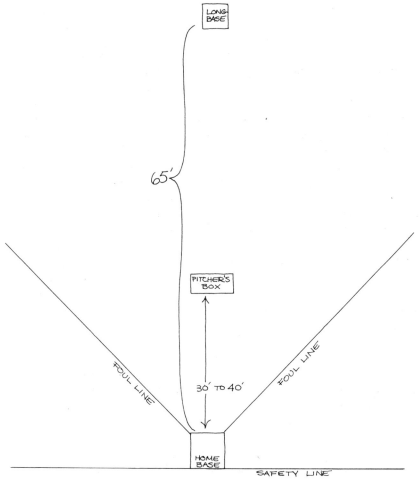

Figure 10—8. Playing area for Long Ball.

Two teams alternate as batters and fielders. Each member of the batting team, in succession, bats the ball and runs to long base. If it is a fair hit, he tries to run back across the safety line before he is put out by the fielding team; if it was a foul hit, he waits at long base until a succeeding batter makes a fair hit and then tries to run to safety.

If a throwing instead of a batting game is desired, the batters throw the ball through a pitching practice frame, or between two standards placed about 18 inches apart. Contact with any portion of the frame or standards constitutes a foul and the batter runs immediately to long base but no farther. A successfully thrown ball which passes through without contact is a fair ball and the batter may attempt a home run. The substitution of throwing for batting is a good lead-up for Long Ball.

Players are divided into two teams and the members are numbered. Each team may select a pitcher, catcher, and other fielders, or players may rotate to positions with the change of innings.

The player of each team at bat who made the last out during the previous time at bat may be the umpire for the new inning. If it becomes necessary for him to bat, the last runner of the batting team to cross the safety line before the umpire's turn to bat takes over his duties until the official umpire returns home successfully or is put out. He then resumes his umpiring duties for the remainder of the inning. (Umpires could be selected for each game, giving each child an opportunity to have the responsibility of officiating.)

The game is played in innings, or in two equal playing periods for each team, or in one playing period for each team. When the first organization is used, three outs change the inning and an inning is complete when both teams have had a chance at bat. When the second or third organization is used, play continues for the team at bat regardless of outs made until the end of the time period.

A batter must continue at bat until a contact with the ball is made by his bat. The contact may result in (1) foul tip (merely grazing the ball with the bat); (2) a foul ball; or (3) a fair hit. The batter cannot be put out on stikes. The instant a batter contacts the ball, no matter how lightly and regardless of whether the ball is "fair" or "foul," he must drop his bat and run to long base.

A ball which lands outside or behind one of the lines between home plate and first or third is a foul ball. When a foul ball is struck, the batter, if he reaches long base, must remain there until another member of his team makes a fair hit, whereupon he and other members of his team at the long base try to reach and cross the safety line.

A batted ball which lands on or inside the base lines is a fair ball. When a fair hit is made, the batter should attempt a round trip to long base and home across the safety line. At the same time any players at long base should attempt to complete their run. To be legal, each runner must cross the safety line at some point between the two ends of the line without being tagged with the ball by a fielder.

Fielders move about as necesary. Each inning one should be assigned to remain near the long base since runners who lose contact with long base may be tagged by any fielder who holds the ball or who contacts the base with the ball in his hand before the runner reaches it.

When the runner is returning from long base, the fielders should go with them and be ready to receive a thrown ball in an effort to tag out one or more runners before they can cross the safety line.

The batter is out under the following conditions:

1. When a fly ball is caught.
2. When a foul tip is caught.
3. When a runner is thrown out before reaching long base. In order for a runner to be thrown out, the ball must reach the fielder at long base, who, while holding the ball, must then touch long base before the runner reaches the base. Runners cannot be thrown out when trying to cross the safety line. They must be tagged with the ball while it is held in the hand of the fielder.
4. When the runner going to long base or returning to the safety line is tagged with the ball in the hand of a fielder.
5. When a runner at long base, not in contact with the base, is tagged with the ball.
6. When all players of a batting team are held at long base because only foul strikes were made by members of the team.
7. When a batter slings his bat as he starts for long base.

Each time a runner reaches long base and on a fair hit returns successfully over the safety line 1 point is scored. The team with the most points at the conclusion of the playing period is the winner.

MODIFIED SOFTBALL

Objectives: Lead-up game for softball, throwing, catching, running

Area: Playground or activity room with softball diamond

Equipment: Ball, bat, bases

Softball may be simplified by changing the equipment and the size of the playing area and modifying the rules. Plastic balls and bats make the game suitable for indoor areas with reduced space. Other frequently used modifications include punkin baseball, kick baseball, and dodge baseball.

Punkin Baseball is the same as softball, except that a volleyball is used along with a standard bat.

In *Kick Baseball* the pitcher rolls or throws a soccer ball and the batter kicks it. This game is usually played without calling balls or strikes, allowing the batter to wait for a pitch he likes. If played with an umpire who calls balls and strikes, the strike zone differs from that in baseball. A strike is any pitch that crosses the plate below the batter's knees.

Dodge Baseball is the same as softball except that: (a) In addition to the usual methods a base runner can be put out by being hit with a thrown ball while not on base; (b) a fielder is not permitted to run with the ball or hold it at any time, but must throw it immediately, either at a runner or to another fielder. This game, of course, requires a ball that is soft. It is often played with a softball that has become really soft, or with the balls and variations described above.

BEATBALL

Objectives: Lead-up activity for softball, throwing, catching, striking, running

Area: Playground, activity room

Equipment: Ball, bat, bases

Same as softball except that when a batter hits a fair ball that is not caught on the fly he must run the bases in order, making a home run or nothing. The fielders must recover the ball, throw it to first base and then to the other bases in order. At each base the ball must be held by a fielder who is touching the base, and no fielder may run with the ball at any time. The runner is not out until the ball gets home ahead of him. He might appear to be out at second base but get home safely because of a poor throw or catch between second and home.

Variation: A playground ball is rolled to the batter who kicks it or hits it with a bat, and then runs around the bases as above. The fielders must recover the ball and then throw it through a basketball goal to put the runner out. When the basket is made before the runner touches all four bases, he is out.

TETHERBALL

Objectives: Striking, development of eye-hand coordination

Area: Playground or activity room with tetherball court

Equipment: Pole and tetherball

A vertical pole 10 feet high is firmly planted in the ground or attached to a broad, heavy base. One end of a strong cord 7½ feet long is attached to the top of the pole and a ball—which may be a tennis ball enclosed in a net cover or a leather-covered ball made for the game—is attached to the other end. A line is marked around the pole 6 feet above the ground. A circle 6 feet in diameter is marked on the ground with the pole as the center, a diameter of the circle is extended in both directions to make a line 20 feet long. Two service spots are marked on the ground 6 feet from the pole, the imaginary line connecting these spots being perpendicular to the long line and passing through the center of the base of the pole. The game is usually played with wooden paddles like those used in paddle tennis. If a larger ball is used, striking with the fist replaces the paddles.

Each of two players stands on one side of the long line. The object is to strike the ball in such a way as to cause the cord to wrap around the pole above the line at the 6 foot mark and to continue doing so until the cord is completely wrapped around the pole.

The first server is determined by some manner and he gets his choice of directions in which to wind the cord. He stands on his service spot and bats the ball. Thereafter either player may bat the ball whenever he can reach it without touching or stepping over the long line, or stepping into the 6-foot circle. Play continues until one player has won by winding the cord completely around the pole, unless a foul is committed. In case of a foul, play is stopped and the opponent is permitted to serve the ball.

VOLLEYBALL SKILLS

NEWCOMB

Objectives: Lead-up activity for volleyball, catching, throwing, striking

Area: Playground or activity room with volleyball standards

Equipment: Net, volleyball

Newcomb is essentially the same as volleyball, except that the ball must always be caught and thrown rather than batted. The ball must always be caught cleanly. If a player misses or juggles the ball, his team loses the point. The best way to play the game is to follow the rules of volleyball. Newcomb is often used as a lead-up game for teaching volleyball and is not suited to skilled players. The following variations are most commonly used:

1. The player who catches the ball when it comes over the net must return it over the net with passing to a teammate prohibited. This variation is not used if the game is a lead-up to volleyball. The ball may be caught on the fly or after one bounce.

2. Same as the above form, except that play is always started with volleyball serve.

3. If an ordinary fence or tennis court is used instead of a net, the court should be as wide as possible and much shallower than a volleyball court, requiring the players to run rapidly back and forth along the fence. This variation should be played without passing to teammates and in some situations it may be wise to have a neutral zone extending a short distance from the fence.

MODIFIED VOLLEYBALL

Objectives: Lead-up activity for volleyball, striking, development of eye-hand coordination

Area: Playground or activity room with volleyball standards

Equipment: Net, volleyball

Volleyball is sometimes modified in various ways to meet special situations without changing its essential nature. The official rules specify a net 7½ feet high for play by women; it is recommended that a net of this height or even lower be used whenever it seems more suited to the abilities of the players.

The game is sometimes played with more than six on a team. This may result in an undesirable reduction in the activity of the players or may cause the acitvity to be unequally distributed. For inexperienced players the limit of two passes may be eliminated, and it is sometimes useful to require two passes or more. The variations, giant volleyball and bounce volleyball, described below, are recommended.

Giant Volleyball is Volleyball played with a cageball 36 inches in diameter or as large as available. Something sturdier than a net is required; for example, a row of parallel bars. If a net is used, it should be lowered to 6 feet or less. The server has two chances and any serve may be assisted once. There is no limit on the number of passes. There is also no limit on the number of players on a team; six is hardly enough and the game does very well with 20.

Bounce Volleyball is the same as Volleyball, except that every time the ball is hit it must bounce on the floor before the next man plays it. The serve must strike the floor on the server's side and bounce over the net, which is lowered for this variation. A pass from one man to a teammate must bounce between them. A ball that goes over the net must bounce over.

REFERENCES AND SOURCES

Bancroft, Jesse: *Games.* New York: Macmillan, 1937.

Bucher, C. A., and Reade, E. M.: *Physical Education and Health in the Elementary School.* New York: Macmillan, 1964.

Clarke, H. H., and Haar, F. B.: *Health and Physical Education for the Elementary School Classroom Teacher.* Englewood Cliffs, N.J.: Prentice-Hall, 1964.

Donnelly, Richard, Helms, William G., and Mitchell, Elmer D.: *Active Games and Contests,* 2nd ed. New York: Ronald Press, 1958.

Farina, A. M., Furth, S. H., and Smith, J. M. *Growth Through Play.* Englewood Cliffs, N.J.: Prentice-Hall, 1959.

Harbin, E. O.: *The Fun Encyclopedia.* Nashville: Abingdon Press, 1960.

Hindman, D. A.: *The Complete Book of Games and Stunts.* Englewood Cliffs, N.J.: Prentice-Hall, 1956.

How We Do It Game Book. Washington, D.C.: American Association for Health, Physical Education and Recreation, 1964.

Thompson, G. G.: *Child Psychology: Growth Trends in Psychological Adjustment,* 2nd ed. Boston, Houghton-Mifflin, 1962.

Van Dalen, W., Dexter, G., and Williams, J. F.: *Physical Education in the Elementary School.* Sacramento: California State Department of Education, 1951.

CHAPTER **11**

Rhythms

Every movement that we make has both spatial and temporal aspects. The temporal aspects are based on rhythms which are many in form, ranging from exotic dances to the basic beats of drums and other simple instruments. Further observation will indicate that rhythm is present in walking, running, throwing and all other skilled movements. Rhythmic activities may be used to facilitate exploration and various other forms of body awareness. Self-expression may also be fulfilled through the use of rhythmic activities which emphasizes the uniqueness of the individual and his own integration.

The purpose of this chapter is not to describe the rhythm that can be observed in skilled motor patterns, but to suggest ways in which games and activities using a "beat" or musical basis may be incorporated into a program designed to teach physical skills to mentally retarded children.

Carey (1960), Joseph and Heimlich (1959), Murphy (1958), Rowland (1965), O'Toole (1962), Weber (1965), and Weigi (1959) have reported some successful methods of teaching rhythm to children with varying degrees of mental retardation. I have achieved the same success using rhythmical activities and music to reach children who were previously insulated from the class activities. This has been true whether the instruction revolved around movement and related activities or immobility and relaxation. The range of activities included under the general heading of rhythms is quite broad and the devices used with success range from the simple to the very complex and sophisticated. The addition of rhythm and music to movement can provide variety, minimize inhibitions, and stimulate creativity.

The teacher of physical education for mentally retarded children is most interested in forms of rhythmics that include movement to fundamental rhythms, games set to music, action songs, and various forms of dance. The remainder of this chapter will describe activities of this nature appropriate for use with retarded children and suggest some story records that may be used to teach retarded children how to listen to music and instructions.

FUNDAMENTAL RHYTHMS

Fundamental rhythms are used to stimulate the child to perform basic movements, either locomotor patterns such as running, walking, and jumping or non-locomotor movements such as stretching, twisting, and flexing. Fundamental rhythms incorporate rhythmic patterns, measures, phrasing, tempo, and accent. The rhythmic pattern is formed from a definite grouping of sounds or beats that is related to an underlying beat. Measures, with the meter of time, provide this underlying beat. Phrasing refers to the group of measures which completes the sequence of sounds or beats. Tempo is the rate of speed, fast, slow, or moderate, at which the beats are made and accent refers to the force of emphasis given to certain beats in the series of beats contained within a measure. Rhythm is initially acquired by having the children associate the rhythmic duration of various notes with their movement experiences.

Name	Symbol	Tempo
Whole note	𝅝	A note to hold
Half note	𝅗𝅥	Slow walk or step, bend
Quarter note	𝅘𝅥	Walking
Eighth note	𝅘𝅥𝅮	Running
Sixteenth note	𝅘𝅥𝅯	Quick shuffle

When the notes are used in sequence or various combinations, it is possible to develop any desired rhythmical pattern. Examples of these patterns are as follows:

Even rhythms

$\frac{4}{4}$	♩ ♩ ♩ ♩ | ♩ ♩ ♩ ♩	walking
$\frac{2}{4}$	♫ ♫ | ♫ ♫	running
$\frac{2}{4}$	♬ ♬ | ♬ ♬	shuffle
$\frac{2}{4}$	♩ ♩ | ♩ ♩	jumping
$\frac{2}{4}$	♩̇ ♩̇ | ♩̇ ♩̇	leaping

Uneven rhythms

6 8	♩ ♪ ♩ ♪ ♩ ♪ ♩ ♪	step-hop
2 4	♪♫ ♪♫ ♪♫ ♪♫	skipping
6 8	♪ ♩ ♪ ♩ ♪ ♩ ♪ ♩ ♪	gallop or swing
3 8	♪ ♩ ♪ ♩ ♪ ♩ ♪ ♩	

bend down, jump up, bend down, jump up.

3 4	♩ ♩ ♩ ♩ ♩ ♩ ♩.	swinging and swaying

Sounds serve to emphasize these fundamental rhythms. Simple isolated sounds, such as clapping or a drum beat, are used initially to teach the fundamental beat of the movement; recordings may be used later to provide variety and opportunities for creative movement. After the teacher has presented the rhythmic pattern or music, the children may follow by clapping on every beat, using various instruments to provide the beat and stepping or using other means of locomotion in conjunction to beats. A ball can be bounced to the beat or non-locomotor activities such as stretching or swaying can be introduced. The basic rhythm instruments that can be easily acquired and used by the teacher or students include:

tom-tom drum	snare drum	tambourine	wood (or tone) block
cymbals	triangle	wrist bells	jingle bells (on stick)
cowbell	conga drum	bongo drum	claves (rhythm sticks)
maracas	gong	finger cymbals	castanets (on handle)
jingle clogs			

Directions for constructing rhythm instruments are given in Chapter 12.

The following records are also useful in various rhythmic activities:

Company	Title	Activity
RCA Basic R. I	"Ballet" (Gluck)	Running
RCA Basic R. I	"Barcarolle" (Rubinstein)	Skipping or gallop
Ruth Evans Records	"Childhood Rhythms, Album I"	Directions in album
RCA Basic R. I	"Galloping Horses" (Anderson)	Gallop
RCA Basic R. I	"Gnomes" (Reinhold)	Tiptoe
RCA Basic R. I	"High Stepping Horses" (Anderson)	Giant steps
C. R. Guild 1012	"Indoors When It Rains"	Directions on record
C. R. Guild 1019	"My Playful Scarf"	Directions on record
Young People's R. 742	"Out-of-Doors"	Directions on record
Children's Music Center	"Rhythmic Activities Album" (Bassett & Chestnut)	Directions in album

RCA Basic R. I	"Sparks" (Moszkowski)	Running, hopping
C. R. Guild 1010	"Sunday in the Park"	Directions on record
C. R. Guild 1017	"Visit to My Little Friend"	Directions on record
RCA Adventures I	"Walking Song" (Thompson)	Walking
RCA Victor	Library for Elementary Schools, Vols. 1 & 2	Variety of tempos
Bowmar 395	Basic Motor and Ball Skills	Locomotor and ball skills
Bowmar 023	Rhythm Time #1	Locomotor activities
Bowmar 024	Rhythm Time #2	Locomotor activities
Horton CC615	The Rhythms Hour	Variety of tempos
Educ. Activities HYP 29	Rhythms for Today	Locomotor activities
Educ. Activities K3090	Fundamental Rhythms	Variety of tempos
Educ. Activities HYP7	Basic Rhythms	Variety of tempos
Educ. Activities EALP 601	Basic Concepts Through Dance	Body image
Educ. Activities K 1066	Kimbo Kids—Rhythmics—Grades 2 and 3	Directions with record
Kimbo 2060	Physical Funness—Rhythmics	Variety of tempos

Kimbo Listening and Moving Series: EA 605, The development of body awareness and position in space; EA 655, Relaxation; EA 606-7, Developing perceptual motor needs of primary level children; EA 657, Dynamic balancing activities; EA 658, Dynamic balancing activities (balance beam activities); EA 656, Simple agility movements for impulse control (pre-tumbling skills).

SINGING GAMES AND SONG STORIES

Singing games add another dimension to the play of children. The music adds rhythmic beat and increases the children's interest in the activity. The games may be a source of creative body movement, using the imagination or concepts gained from other instruction. For example, the children may pretend they are trees that sway from side to side in winds of varying intensity. Other singing games may involve imitation of activities the children observe in daily life, such as washing the dishes or sweeping with brooms. Some records that may be used in singing games are:

Company	Title	Type
Audio-Ed. ABC 3	"Jocko, The Dancing Monkey"	Action song story
Decca CU102	"Genie, The Magic Record"	Song story
Bowmar 1513 B	"Kitty White"	Action song story
Audio-Ed. ABC AS 23	"Traditional Singing Games"	Action song story
Bowmar 1512 A	"Our Exercises"	Action song story
Bowmar	"Singing Games, Album 2"	Action song story
Decca CU-100	"Mother Goose Songs"	Song story
Decca CU-101	"Nursery Rhymes"	Song story
Decca CUS-10	"Shoemaker and the Elves"	Song story
Capitol JOA-3251	"Woody Woodpecker and His Talent Show" and others	Song story
Decca CUS-9	"Goldilocks and the Three Bears"	Song story
Bowmar 1511 A	"Did You Ever See a Lassie"	Singing game

Bowmar 1511 B	"Farmer in the Dell"	Singing game
Bowmar 1513 A	"When I Was a Shoemaker"	Singing game
Bowmar 1512 A	"Little Polly Flinders"	Singing game
Bowmar 1513 B	"Mulberry Bush"	Singing game
Bowmar 1514 A	"Pussy Cat"	Singing game
Bowmar 011	Songs for Children with Special Needs, Record #1	Action song story
Bowmar 012	Songs for Children with Special Needs, Record #2	Action song story
Hoctor CC606	Singing Games	Singing games
Educ. Activities HYP507	Singing Action Games	Action songs
Educ. Activities HYP508	Action Songs and Rounds	Singing games
Kimbo CM1025	Creative Music for Exceptional Children	Singing games
Kimbo CM1021	Rhythms and Songs for Exceptional Children	Folk songs

Rhythmical Activities (Series I) by Frances R. Stuart and John S. Ludlam with musical arrangements by Earl Juhas, Burgess Publishing Company, 426 South Sixth Street, Minneapolis, Minnesota.

MUSICAL STORIES

Listening is vital in most aspects of education, and physical education is no exception. Furthermore, listening is involved in all avenues of musical activity, the fundamental rhythms, story games or singing games, and action songs. An excellent tool for teaching retarded children to listen to the music or beat is the variety of musical stories available on records. Sounds that exist in the environment around the school may also be used in this manner. The fire siren, the singing of the birds, the "tick-tock" of clocks, footsteps, tapping on various surfaces, and the sounds made by a wide variety of other activities provide ample stimulus for listening experiences. Since the attention span of the retarded child is relatively short, the teacher must avoid lengthy recordings that are played at one sitting. The teacher must determine the optimum length of time in terms of the maturation and past experience of his students. It may be wise to begin with musical stories and similar activities in sessions of only four to six minutes.

The following list of musical story records suggests some of the materials now available:

Company	Title
Children's Record Guild, 208	"Pinocchio"
Capitol, L-3007	"Rusty in Orchestraville"
Columbia, ML-4038	"Peter and the Wolf" (Serge Prokofiev)
Musicraft, M-77	"Peer Gynt and the Trolls" (Edvard Grieg)

Children's Record	"Cinderella" (Serge Prokofiev)
Guild, 201	
Decca, CU-106	"Tubby the Tuba"
RCA Victor	Basic Listening Program, Volumes 1—6
Children's Record	"Train to the Zoo"
Guild, 1001	
Children's Record	"Four Bears"
Guild, 1009	
Children's Record	"The Merry Toy Shop"
Guild, 1022	
Bowmar 029	Listening Time #1
Bowmar 030	Listening Time #2
Bowmar 031	Listening Time #3

While these records are suggested as aids in teaching children how to listen, they may, of course, be used later as a springboard for other activity. Once the children have learned the stories, action plays based on the characters in the story may provide the means for increased physical activity.

SIMPLE DANCES

A natural outgrowth of the activities described in this chapter would be instruction in simple dances and dance-like activities. Once the child has learned to listen to the music, to perform simple motor activities to music, and to attend to music for longer periods of time, gross body movements set to music in the form of dance are within his grasp. Record albums with both music and directions for simple dances are provided by a large number of companies. The following musical scores and written descriptions of simple dances and mixers have been used successfully with retarded children. Where records are available, the number and company supplying the album is indicated along with the musical score.

OH, WHERE IS MY LITTLE DOG?

tail ____ cut long, Oh where, oh where has he gone?

Formation: Single-circle formation, all holding hands and facing center. Two children are in center of circle—one the master, the other the little dog.

Step: Walk.

Measures 1-4: Players circle counter-clockwise, singing verse. Master shades eyes looking for little dog. Little dog on all fours hops around inside of circle, barking.

Measures 5-6: Players stop, then begin to circle clockwise, continuing verse. Master makes fists on his head indicating the short ears; then indicates long tail by waving one arm behind his back.

Measures 7-8: Circle continues clockwise; master continues to look for dog, using hand as visor; little dog barks.

(From Albert M. Farina, Sol H. Furth, and Joseph M. Smith: GROWTH THROUGH PLAY, © 1959. Reprinted by permission of Prentice-Hall, Inc., Englewood Cliffs, N. J.)

DID YOU EVER SEE A LASSIE (LADDIE)?

Record: RCA Victor 21618

Did you ev - er see a las - sie, a las - sie, a las - sie? Did you ev - er see a las - sie do this way and that? Do ____ this way and that way, and this way and that way. Did you ev - er see a las - sie do this way and that?

Formation: Single circle, facing left, hands joined. One child is in the center.

Step: Walk.

Dance: Dancers walk to the left eight steps, then turn and walk eight steps to the right. As they sing line three, the child in the center does any action the children can imitate. On line four, they all imitate the action. Select a new child for the center and repeat.

(From Albert M. Farina, Sol H. Furth, and Joseph M. Smith: GROWTH THROUGH PLAY,©1959. Reprinted by permission of Prentice-Hall, Inc., Englewood Cliffs, N.J.)

FARMER IN THE DELL

Record: Victor 21618 Album 87

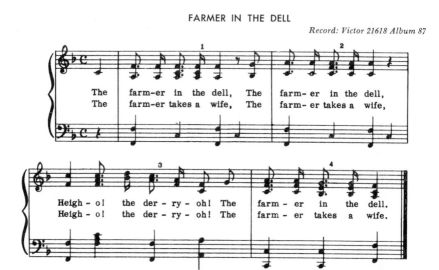

Formation: Single circle, children holding hands, farmer (chosen by leader) standing in center of circle.

Step: A counter-clockwise walk.

Verse I: Children sing first verse while moving counter-clockwise around the farmer.

Verse II et seq.: In the second verse, the farmer beckons another child from the outer circle, who stands by the farmer. The circle keeps moving while each verse is sung, and each time the player last called into the circle beckons another child until all eight characters are standing within the circle.

Repeat Verses: After the last verse when the rat has taken the cheese, the game continues in reverse, with each of the center players "running away." Thus, beginning with the *farmer* and proceeding to the *cheese*, each player returns to the outer circle.

Final Verse: After all players except the cheese have returned to the circle, the players sing "The cheese stands alone," shaking their fingers at the *cheese*.

The following verses change only in the choice in each, and continue in this order:

> The wife takes a child, etc.
> The child takes a nurse, etc.
> The nurse takes a dog, etc.
> The dog takes a cat, etc.
> The cat takes a rat, etc.
> The rat takes the cheese, etc.

After the cheese is selected, the verses are repeated in the same order, only the following verse is sung for each player returning to the circle.

> The farmer runs away,
> The farmer runs away,
> Heigh-o! the derry-oh!
> The farmer runs away.

The above verse is sung for all the characters until the "cheese is standing alone." At this point the last verse is sung, with the players in the circle pointing a finger at the poor cheese.

> The cheese stands alone,
> The cheese stands alone,
> Heigh-o! the derry-oh!
> The cheese stands alone.

(From Albert M. Farina, Sol H. Furth, and Joseph M. Smith: GROWTH THROUGH PLAY, © 1959. Reprinted by permission of Prentice-Hall, Inc., Englewood Cliffs, N. J.)

ATISKET ATASKET

Formation: Single circle, facing center, players standing still and holding hands. One player who has been chosen to be "it" is on the outside of the circle.

Step: Skip or run.

Action: Player on outside of circle skips around circle carrying a kerchief and singing the verse with the rest of the players.

The last line is repeated *only* by the "it" player until he reaches the one behind whom he wishes to drop the kerchief or other object. He says, "It is you!" and immediately starts on a quick run around the circle.

The player behind whom the kerchief has been dropped picks it up and at once starts around the circle in the opposite direction, the object being to see which of the two shall first reach the vacant place. The one who is left out takes the kerchief for the next game.

Should a player fail to discover that the kerchief has been dropped behind him until the "it" has completed a turn around the circle, the player must give up his position in the circle to the "it."

(From Albert M. Farina, Sol H. Furth, and Joseph M. Smith: GROWTH THROUGH PLAY, © 1959. Reprinted by permission of Prentice-Hall, Inc., Englewood Cliffs, N. J.)

TEN LITTLE INDIANS

Formation: Classroom, with the ten little Indian boys or girls standing in one corner of the room or outside of the room.

Action: While singing the first verse, the children appear one by one as their numbers are being called. In the second verse the order of numbers is reversed, so that the children disappear one by one.

This may also be played with the children using their fingers.

(From Albert M. Farina, Sol H. Furth, and Joseph M. Smith: GROWTH THROUGH PLAY, © 1959. Reprinted by permission of Prentice-Hall, Inc., Englewood Cliffs, N. J.)

I'M A LITTLE TEAPOT

Formation: Standing in classroom.

Measures 1-3: Place one hand on top of head, elbow out to the side.

Measure 4: Extend the other arm out to side.

Measures 5-8: Bend body to side so that the spout is bending towards the floor.

(From Albert M. Farina, Sol H. Furth, and Joseph M. Smith: GROWTH THROUGH PLAY, © 1959. Reprinted by permission of Prentice-Hall, Inc., Englewood Cliffs, N.J.)

TWINKLE, TWINKLE, LITTLE STAR

Formation: Rank.

Step: Tip-toe steps.

Measures 1-4: Children hold arms to the front and wriggle fingers while singing.

Measures 5-6: With both arms circling overhead, they turn to right and take seven tip-toe steps.

Measures 7-8: Arms out to front, they wriggle fingers.

Measures 9-10: Both arms circling overhead, they turn to left and take seven tip-toe steps.

Measures 11-12: They wriggle fingers, with both arms to the front.

(From Albert M. Farina, Sol H. Furth, and Joseph M. Smith: GROWTH THROUGH PLAY, © 1959. Reprinted by permission of Prentice-Hall, Inc., Englewood Cliffs, N. J.)

THE MULBERRY BUSH

Formation: Single circle formation holding hands.

Step: Walk.

Action: Children sing first verse while walking around circle in counter-clockwise direction. With the other verses they dramatize the action of the verse, i.e., "This is the way we *scrub the floor.*" On the last line of each verse, "So early in the morning," the children spin around, each in his own place.

> 3. This is the way we iron our clothes . . .
>   So early Tuesday morning.
> 4. This is the way we scrub the floor . . .
>   So early Wednesday morning.
> 5. This is the way we mend our clothes . . .
>   So early Thursday morning.

6. This is the way we sweep the house . . .
   So early Friday morning.
7. Thus we play when our work is done . . .
   So early Saturday morning.

(From Albert M. Farina, Sol H. Furth, and Joseph M. Smith: GROWTH THROUGH PLAY, © 1959. Reprinted by permission of Prentice-Hall, Inc., Englewood Cliffs, N. J.)

HICKORY DICKORY DOCK

Record: Folkcraft V22760

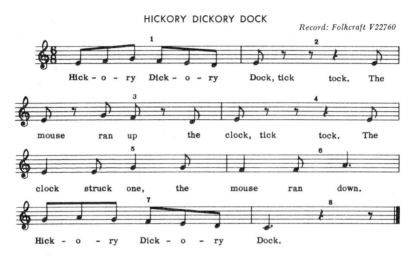

Formation: Single circle or rank formation.

Line 1: Raising hands above the head, children sway to left and then to right, as pendulums. They stamp feet, left and then right on "tick" and "tock."

Line 2: They bring hands down to waist, then climb again as mouse runs up the clock. At the words "tick tock," children stamp feet once left, once right.

Line 3: Children hold left hand to left ear on "the clock struck one." They raise right hand, holding one finger in the air to indicate the time. The mouse runs down as both hands creep downward to the waist.

Line 4: Raising hands above head, children sway left and right as pendulums.

(From Albert M. Farina, Sol H. Furth, and Joseph M. Smith: GROWTH THROUGH PLAY, © 1959. Reprinted by permission of Prentice-Hall, Inc., Englewood Cliffs, N. J.)

SING A SONG OF SIXPENCE
(England)

Record: RCA Victor 22760

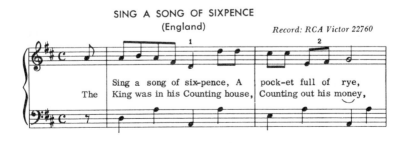

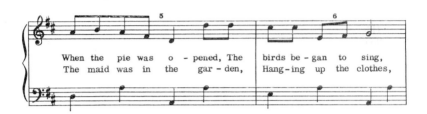

Formation: Single circle, facing center with hands joined.

Step: Walk.

Measures 1-2: Players walk around circle briskly, swinging arms.

Measures 3-4: Walk toward center; squat on heels.

Measure 5: Stand up.

Measure 6: Snap fingers, holding hands high.

Measure 7: Walk backward to original places.

Measure 8: Bow or curtsy on "King."

Verse II

Measures 1-8: Players stand in circle formation, suiting action to the words.

Note: For the second verse select a King, Queen, and Maid and have them standing in the center of the circle imitating their respective parts.

POP GOES THE WEASEL

Records: F 1007 RCA Victor 20151
—M104 Folkcraft V20151

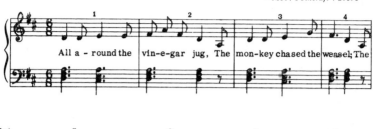

All a - round the vin-e-gar jug, The mon-key chased the weasel; The

mon-key pulled the stop - per out, Pop goes the weas - el!

Pen - ny for a spool___ of thread, Pen -ny for a need-le;

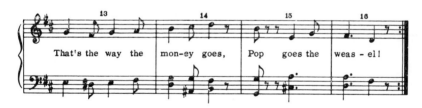

That's the way the mon-ey goes, Pop goes the weas - el!

Formation: Players form double circle, facing clockwise, the girls on the outside.

Step: Walk.

Measures 1-4: All walk eight steps forward.

Measures 5-6: Partners join inside hands and face each other. The girl turns under the raised joined hands and the boy stands still.

Measures 7-8: Partners drop hands; the boy bows and the girl curtsies.

Measures 9-12: All walk 8 steps forward.

Measures 13-14: Partners again face while boy turns under raised joined hands.

Measures 15-16: Dropping hands, the boy bows and the girl curtsies.

(From Albert M. Farina, Sol H. Furth, and Joseph M. Smith: GROWTH THROUGH PLAY, © 1959. Reprinted by permission of Prentice-Hall, Inc., Englewood Cliffs, N. J.)

SHOO FLY
(United States)

Record: Decca 18222

Formation: Couples in single circle facing center, hands joined, gents on right.

Step: Walk, swing, and promenade.

Measures 1-2: Four steps to center.

Measures 3-4: Four steps back, drop hands.

Measures 5-8: Repeat.

Measures 9-12: Swing partners with 8 skips.

Measures 13-16: In skating position, promenade 8 steps counter-clockwise. Repeat.

(From Albert M. Farina, Sol H. Furth, and Joseph M. Smith: GROWTH THROUGH PLAY, © 1959. Reprinted by permission of Prentice-Hall, Inc., Englewood Cliffs, N. J.)

LOOBY LOO
(England)

Record: RCA Victor 20214

Oh! Here we dance loo-by loo,___ Oh! Here we dance loo-by light, Oh!
Here we dance loo-by loo,___ All on a sum-mer's___ night. I
put my right hand in, I put my right hand out, I
give my right hand a shake, shake, shake, And turn my-self a-bout.

2. Put my left hand in, etc.
3. Put my right foot in, etc.
4. Put my left foot in, etc.
5. Put my head way in, etc.
6. Put my whole self in, etc.

Formation: Single circle, facing center, all hands joined.

Step: Skip or walk.

Chorus:

Measures 1-3: Skip around circle, swinging arms freely.

Measure 4: Dropping hands, children turn around in place and finish facing center.

Verses 1-5: Pantomime the words. Repeat chorus after each verse.

Variation: Players advance toward center of circle on first and third lines of the chorus and return on the second and fourth, game continuing as before.

(From Albert M. Farina, Sol H. Furth, and Joseph M. Smith: GROWTH THROUGH PLAY, © 1959. Reprinted by permission of Prentice-Hall, Inc., Englewood Cliffs, N. J.)

BINGO

Formation: Double-circle, boys on inside, girls on outside.

Steps and Figures: Promenade, grand right and left, slide.

Measures 1-16: Taking partner in promenade position, walk 16 solemn steps counter-clockwise.

Measures 17-22: Couples turn in and face center. All join hands to form a single circle. Starting on right foot, all take 12 slides sideways.

Measures 23-24: Still keeping in single-circle formation, turn and face partner for "grand-right-and-left."

Action on spoken words: Shake partner's right hand and say "B." Pass partner by and take left hand of the next and say "I." Continue in this manner for "N," "G," and "O." Those holding hands on "O!" are now partners.

(From Albert M. Farina, Sol H. Furth, and Joseph M. Smith: GROWTH THROUGH PLAY, © 1959. Reprinted by permission of Prentice-Hall, Inc., Englewood Cliffs, N. J.)

EENSEY WEENSEY SPIDER

Up came the sun, And dried up all the rain. And the

een - sey ween-sey spid - er, Climbed up the spout a - gain.

Formation: Classroom.

Measures 1-2: Pivot right thumb and left index finger, left thumb and right index finger, alternately from waist to forehead.

Measures 3-4: Bring hands slowly down. Bring hands to the side.

Measures 5-6: Raise hands above the head. Bring hands out to the side.

Measures 7-8: Repeat the first movement at the start of the verse.

(From Albert M. Farina, Sol H. Furth, and Joseph M. Smith: GROWTH THROUGH PLAY,, © 1959. Reprinted by permission of Prentice-Hall, Inc., Englewood Cliffs, N. J.)

SUMMARY

Rhythm, which is present in all skilled motor activities, forms the basis of the temporal aspects of movement. Consequently, rhythmic activities may be used by the teacher to facilitate movement and awareness in the retarded child. Rhythmic patterns may be used to stimulate basic movement and non-locomotor patterns. Singing games and story songs, musical stories, and simple dances also add dimension to the physical education programs for retarded children. Rhythmic activities are an integral part of the physical education program.

REFERENCES

Carey, Margretta: Music for the educable mentally retarded. *Musical Educ. J.* 46:72, 1960.

Doll, Edna, and Nelson, Mary Jarman: *Rhythms Today!* Morristown, N.J.: Silver Burdett Company, 1965.

Dobbs, J. P. B.: *The Slow Learner and Music: A Handbook for Teachers.* London: Oxford University Press, 1966.

Farina, Albert M., Furth, Sol H., and Smith, Joseph M.: *Growth Through Play.* Englewood Cliffs, N. J.: Prentice-Hall, 1959.

Garretson, Robert L.: *Music in Childhood Education.* New York: Appleton-Century-Crofts, 1966.

Joseph, Harry, and Heimlich, Evelyn P.: The therapeutic use of music with "treatment resistant" children. *Amer. J. Ment. Defic.* 64:41–49, 1959.

Kaplan, Max, and Steiner, Frances J.: *Musicianship for the Classroom Teacher.* Chicago: Rand McNally and Company, 1966.

Murphy, Mary M.: A large scale music therapy program for institutionalized low grade and middle defectives. *Amer. J. Ment. Defic.* 63:268–273, 1958.

Rowland, Hershel: Much alike: a little different. *Musical Educ. J.* 51:93–94, 1965.

Runkle, Aleta, and Eriksen, Mary LeBow: *Music for Today's Boys and Girls: Sequential Learning through the Grades.* Boston: Allyn and Bacon, 1966.

O'Toole, Catherine M.: Music for the handicapped child. *Musical Educ. J.* 48:73–76, 1962.

Timmerman, Maurine: *Let's Teach Music in the Elementary School.* Evanston, Ill.: Summy-Birchard Company, 1958.

Weber, Richard: Music for exceptional children. *Musical Educ. J.* 51:112, 1965.

Weigi, Vally: Functional music: a therapeutic tool in working with the mentally retarded. *Amer. J. Ment. Defic.* 63:672–678, 1959.

CHAPTER **12**

Equipment Ideas

Throughout this book I have emphasized the idea that although the need for varied physical activity is present in all children, it is critical to the development of mentally retarded children. Not only do retarded children have intellectual deficits and impaired behavior, but they also frequently exhibit complicating factors such as a lack of coordination and perceptual-motor skills, lowered resistance to fatigue resulting from lower levels of strength and poor body mechanics, and an apparent lack of motivation. These physical defects most often result from the reduced activity levels observed in these children (AAHPER, 1966).

Therefore, a program of activities must be developed to enable the retarded child to acquire adequate levels of strength and endurance, to master fundamental motor skills such as walking and climbing, and to develop appropriate combinations of basic large muscle movements that can be refined through increased practice and the use of appropriate small muscles. Furthermore, the child needs ample opportunity to participate in activities that enable him to develop a concept of himself; he must be able to continually test his abilities and determine which skills he can perform and which are unattainable.

Inasmuch as adaptive behavior refers to the effectiveness with which an individual copes with the natural and social demands of his environment, physical activities play a central role in the child's development. Physical competence enables the child to move through his environment; his activities allow him to manipulate objects and learn about them, to develop many self-help and safety skills, and to master occupationally-related skills that may be used in workshops and other vocational agencies. Since the need is to provide physical activity that is individualized, progressive, varied, and self-testing, apparatus must be developed for specific activity patterns. Some agencies have purchased ready-made equipment while others have relied upon equipment built to their specifications. This chapter will describe equipment that may be constructed by parents or teachers to implement the physical education of retarded children.

OBSTACLE COURSE

One type of activity program especially effective for the retarded child is the obstacle course which contains equipment requiring a variety of movement patterns. The ideal obstacle course includes equipment that is adaptable to children with varying levels of proficiency. It should also make the child aware of his progression through the program, require a large variety of motor responses and enable the child to test his motor abilities. An obstacle course may be constructed on a limited budget from a wide range of available materials. Natural objects such as trees, discarded objects such as auto tires or drainage tiles, and building materials such as pipe, rope, lumber, and telephone poles may be used effectively.

The obstacle course must be designed to include activities that require the child to use all parts of his body. Each obstacle should generate as wide a variety of motor responses as is possible. The obstacle course which was developed for Camp Courage, the residential summer camp sponsored by the Lucas County, Ohio, Association for Retarded Children will illustrate the type of equipment especially useful in these activities. Although these items were mostly custom built, similar pieces of equipment are available commercially.

Arm and Shoulder Strength Development

Entry into workshops and other occupational skills programs often depends on the development of adequate levels of strength and endurance in the arm and shoulder girdle. Obstacles which require the use of the arms and supply resistance through the use of body weight are used to achieve this objective. The obstacle depicted in Figure 12—1 requires the child to either hang on the rope or attempt to climb the rope. The activity is geared to the child's strength performance and he is gradually directed to go on to an activity that requires more strength. Figure 12—2 displays an obstacle on which the children can hang, then swing from an elevated platform and then release, dropping to the lower level. The activities performed on this obstacle can be modified as for the first.

For children who do not have sufficient strength and endurance to lift their body weight, an obstacle was designed to minimize the strength required. Children using the equipment in Figure 12—3 lie on their back on the horizontal beam and either pull or push their body weight, using the rungs of the ladder above for leverage. Once sufficient strength has been developed, the children can go on to more difficult obstacles. The beam on this obstacle must be made of material that is free of splinters or sharp edges.

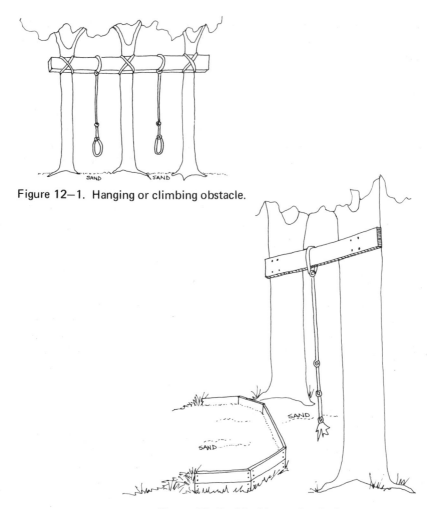

Figure 12—1. Hanging or climbing obstacle.

Figure 12—2. Climbing and swinging obstacle.

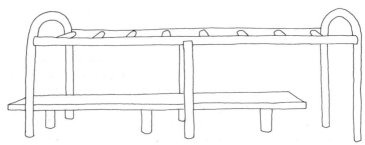

Figure 12—3. Obstacle for developing arm and shoulder strength.

Total Body Development

Obstacles that contribute to the development of total body strength and fitness must involve all parts of the child's body. Most generally, these pieces of equipment require climbing of some kind. The obstacle in Figure 12–4 is the easiest for children to maneuver as the climb is made over an inclined plane. The height and slope of the obstacle will determine its difficulty and it may be constructed from material such as 2 by 6 or 2 by 4 lumber.

Figure 12–4. Climbing ladder.

A more challenging climbing apparatus is constructed for the vertical climb. The obstacle displayed in Figure 12–5 illustrates this type of equip-

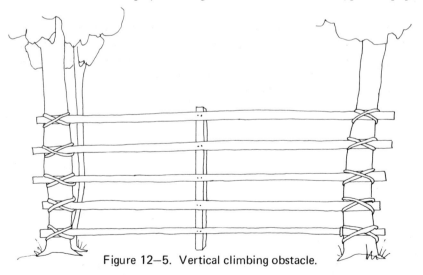

Figure 12–5. Vertical climbing obstacle.

ment. If the rungs are spaced far enough apart, children who are unable to climb over the obstacle can climb between the rungs, increasing its usefulness.

Figure 12–6 illustrates other equipment that may be constructed to promote climbing and other movement activities. The children climb over the rungs or through the holes in the sides to enter the apparatus. This type of equipment may be placed on the playground for imaginative play rather than in an obstacle course. The corner posts should be made from 4 by 4 or comparable lumber, the sides of durable exterior materials, and the rungs secured to prevent their rotating while the children are climbing on them.

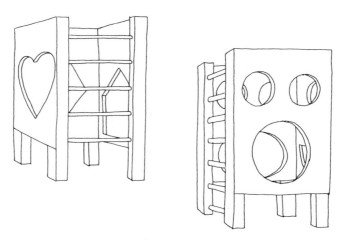

Figure 12–6. Apparatus for climbing over and through.

Crawling

Crawling is a locomotor pattern used in movement as well as an activity that contributes to general body strength and fitness development. The Camp Courage obstacle course uses two sizes of storm sewer tiling as crawling tunnels (see Figure 12–7). Sand, or some similar material is placed on the bottom of the tile to soften the crawling surface.

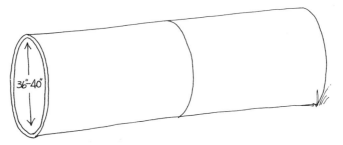

Figure 12–7. Storm sewer tiling for crawling activities.

Large tractor tires may be used for the same purpose. They are buried and secured in concrete as indicated in Figure 12—8. If the tire has large lugs, the children can climb over, as well as through, the tire. These tires màke attractive play equipment when painted bright colors.

Figure 12—8. Large tractor tire mounted
for crawling and climbing.

Balance and Agility

A wide variety of obstacles may be constructed to provide opportunities for balancing and agility. These obstacles range from balance beams constructed from 4 by 4 lumber and logs (see Figure 12—9) and ladders that the children can step on or into (see Figure 12—10) to more elaborately constructed pieces of equipment. The stepping stones or islands shown in Figure 12—11 can be constructed from tree stumps, logs, or pieces of telephone poles. The height of each "island," the distance between them, and the diameter of the individual pieces may be varied as desired.

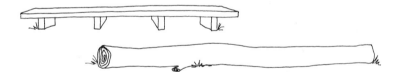

Figure 12—9. Balancing beams and logs.

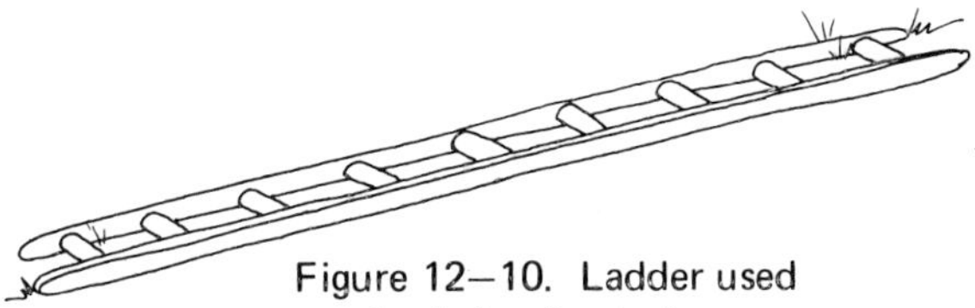

Figure 12—10. Ladder used
for balancing tasks.

Figure 12—11. Stepping stones
made from tree stumps.

Inclined logs or telephone poles (Figure 12–12) provide opportunities for the child to walk up one inclined log and down the log on the opposite side to the ground. This obstacle may be offered with differing degrees of difficulty by changing the slope of the inclined logs.

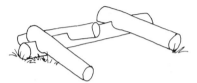

Figure 12–12. Balance obstacle
made with inclined logs.

Telephone poles or logs of differing heights can be buried vertically in the ground close together to provide a balancing and climbing challenge (see Figure 12–13). This piece of equipment may be used in a playground for creative play and free expression rather than as a part of the obstacle course.

Figure 12–13. Climbing obstacle
made from logs.

Discarded automobile and truck tires can be used for the development of balance and agility. When laid in the pattern illustrated in Figure 12–14, children can step from the inside of one tire to the inside of another or walk on the rims. If the child walks on the rims, there is usually enough bend in the rubber to provide a balancing challenge.

Figure 12–14. Balancing obstacle
made from discarded tires.

Course Design

The lay-out of the obstacle course used at Camp Courage is illustrated in Figure 12–15. Note that obstacles requiring large amounts of physical effort are alternated with those items requiring little effort. The course is located in a shady area of the camp some distance from the traditional playground equipment. This allows the camp personnel to conduct many physical activities simultaneously without interference.

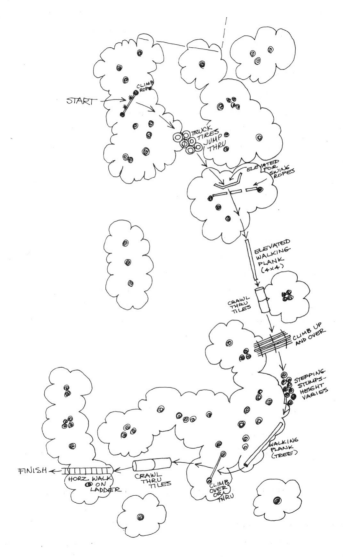

Figure 12–15. Obstacle course at Camp Courage, sponsored by the Lucas County Association for Retarded Children, Ohio.

INDOOR EQUIPMENT

Equipment chosen to aid program implementation should stimulate creativity and imagination as well as provide adventure, social play, and the development of coordination and manipulative skills. Indoor obstacle courses can be constructed with chairs, tables, boxes, and other materials in forms designed to develop overall strength and general physical ability. Other types of equipment developed to meet specific program aims will be described in the areas of balance, rhythms, and basic movement skills.

Balance Equipment

Several types of balance equipment are commercially available and a number of stunts requiring balance skills were noted earlier in Chapter 8. Balance equipment is easily and inexpensively constructed from various pieces of lumber. The four types of balance equipment suggested for inclusion in physical education programs for the handicapped are described in the following paragraphs.

Balance Beam. Balance beams can be constructed from a standard 2 by 4 board in 10-foot lengths. The beams may be used flat on the floor or supports may be made from additional standard 2 by 4 boards that are 6 to 12 inches in length (see Figure 12–16). A T-shaped notch should be cut into the support. The wide part of the cut holds the board so children can walk along the wide side of the board and the narrow part of the cut holds the board on its edge. Three supports are recommended to prevent sag in the middle. Additional pieces of wood may be placed under the supports to improve the appearance or add additional height to the beam.

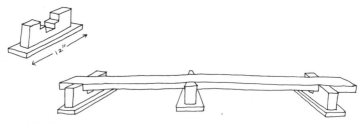

Figure 12–16. Balance beam and support constructed from 2 by 4 lumber.

Balance Board. A balance board is constructed from 3/4 inch plywood or similar material that is from 16 to 24 inches square. A base 3 inches in height is attached to the bottom of the square at the center of the balance board. The size of this base may be 3, 4, 5, or 6 inches in diameter, depending upon the difficulty desired. The base should be attached to the balance board with a bolt that is counter-sunk at both ends (see Figure 12–17).

Figure 12—17. Balance board.

Rocking Board. The platform for a rocking board (Figure 12—18) is made from 3/4 inch plywood or similar material that is 16 by 24 inches in size. A base extending across the 16-inch side is attached to the center of the rocking board. The height and width of the base can be varied to provide rocking boards with differing degrees of difficulty.

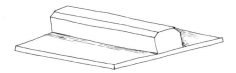

Figure 12—18. Rocking board.

Ridgepole. A ridgepole is constructed with three 1 by 8 inch boards that are 10 feet in length. To construct the ridgepole, place one board flat on the floor and nail the others to it lengthwise to form a compact triangle. The peak of this triangle will be approximately 8 inches above the floor. The student stands on the apparatus with his feet on either side of the ridge and walks along the ridge.

Rhythmic Equipment

A favorite activity of young children is the rhythm band. Fortunately, a wide variety of homemade rhythm equipment can be easily produced and readily assimilated into physical activity. Rhythm instruments that can be made at home include the following:

Drums. Large coffee cans or gallon cans can be converted easily into usable drums. Pieces of rubber inner tube or denim that is folded double can be used to make the drum heads. Belt eyelets can be inserted into the material for the drum heads and then the two heads are laced onto the can with leather strips. If denim is used it should be thoroughly shellacked both before and after the head is attached to the can (see Figure 12—19). The eraser of a pencil can be used as a beater.

Figure 12—19. Homemade drum.

Tambourine. This instrument can be constructed from plywood circles about 8 inches in diameter. Two circles from 1/4-inch plywood that are glued to the top and bottom of 2-inch blocks cut from 3/4-inch material form the frame for the tambourine. Roofing caps are placed in the spaces between the 2-inch blocks by driving a nail through one plywood circle, placing the roofing caps with raised sides together over the end of the nail, and then driving the nail into the other side of the frame. A drum head made from rubber inner tube or shellacked denim can be attached to the tambourine with glue and thumbtacks. This instrument is illustrated in Figure 12—20.

Figure 12—20. Homemade tambourine.

Rhythm Sticks. Painted dowel pins cut in 12-inch sections, or 10- to 12-inch sections of broom handles, make excellent rhythm sticks.

Sand Blocks. Scraps of wood cut into blocks of any desired size can be used for sand blocks. Light sandpaper is cut to fit the width of blocks and is left long enough to overlap the end of the blocks. The sandpaper can be secured to the blocks with either glue or a staple gun. Wooden knobs can be attached to the blocks if desired.

MISCELLANEOUS EQUIPMENT

The following are examples of durable and useful equipment that may be constructed to aid in the development of basic movement skills such as lifting, carrying, and throwing:

Blocks. All sizes of large blocks are easily constructed from economical pieces of lumber. Smaller blocks can be used for eye-hand coordination while larger, heavier blocks are used to teach lifting and carrying and for strength development. The best procedure is to decide on a basic size and then produce whole blocks, half blocks, double blocks, and so on. We have used a 6-inch cube as the basic size successfully. Standard 2 by 4 lumber also may be easily cut into a variety of blocks.

Marble Track. A marble track is constructed from small pieces of molding 18 inches long and light-weight lumber approximately 24 by 2 by 1/4 inches. Three pieces of the light-weight lumber are joined together in a U shape to form each of the two vertical sides of the marble track and four small pieces of molding are attached between the two sides in a zigzag fashion. Space must be provided at each side for the marble to drop from the higher piece of molding into the lower track. The amount of slope in the pieces of molding will determine the speed at which the marbles roll down the track. A larger piece of lumber may be attached to the bottom of the two sides to form a base for the track.

Beanbag Target. A target is constructed from 3/4-inch plywood that is approximately 3 by 4 feet in size. Holes of differing sizes are cut into the target board and the desired design is made. Large sizes are recommended for the holes (see Figure 12—21). A support is attached to the back of the target at each side by hinges and chains are attached between the target and the support to increase stability. Faces may be painted on the target or different shapes may be used for the target holes.

Figure 12—21. Beanbag target.

Ring Toss. The ring toss target is made by attaching a small dowel rod to a circular or square base. Fruit jar rings are used as tossing objects.

Gym Scooters. Good quality pine lumber approximately 2 by 12 by 12 inches in size is used for the scooter body. A 1 1/4-inch caster is attached to each of the four corners of the scooter.

SUMMARY

Retarded children learn through practical experience what objects are like, what they can do, how they react to people, and how people react to them. Skill development, especially in the more severely retarded, is not an automatic process of development; rather, the child must be carefully taught the necessary skills.

Sturdy, imaginative equipment can easily be made by the parent or teacher, following simple directions. Many readily available items can be used to assure program success. The important principle behind any equipment acquisition is that the equipment must fulfill a purpose congruent with the program. If this guideline is followed, the children should profit from the use of a wide variety of equipment that complements a well-developed program.

REFERENCES

Activity Programs for the Mentally Retarded: *J. Health, Phys. Educ., Rec.,* 37:23—38, 1966.

Allen, Marjory (Lady Allen of Hurtwood): *Planning for Play.* Cambridge, Mass.: MIT Press, 1968.

Carter, Joel W.: *How to Make Athletic Equipment.* New York: Ronald Press, 1960.

Frederick, A. Bruce: *212 Ideas for Making Low-cost Physical Education Equipment.* Englewood Cliffs, N.J.: Prentice-Hall, 1963.

Matterson, E.M.: *Play and Playthings for the Preschool Child,* rev. ed. Baltimore: Penguin Books, 1967.

Recreation and Physical Activity for the Mentally Retarded. Washington, D.C.: AAHPER, 1966.

Appendix—Resource Materials

The following list of books and newsletters contains ideas that are of value to teachers of retarded children. These resources have good references for materials to supplement the physical education program content.

NEWSLETTERS

Challenge

Project on Recreation and Fitness for the Mentally Retarded
AAHPER
1201 Sixteenth St., N.W.
Washington, D.C. 20036

ICRH Newsletter

Information Center
Recreation for the Handicapped
Southern Illinois University
Little Grassy Facilities
Carbondale, Illinois 62901

Outlook

AAHPER Unit on Programs for the Handicapped
1201 Sixteenth St., N.W.
Washington, D.C. 20036

BOOKS

Cratty, Bryant J.: *Learning and Playing: Fifty Vigorous Activities for the Atypical Child.* Freeport, N.Y.: Educational Activities, 1968. (Activity cards)

Cratty, Bryant J.: *Development Sequences of Perceptual-Motor Tasks: Movement Activities for Neurologically Handicapped and Retarded Children and Youth.* Freeport, L.I., N.Y.: Educational Activities, Inc., 1967.

Cratty, Bryant J.: *Motor Activity and the Education of Retardates.* Philadelphia: Lea & Febiger, 1969.

Frankel, Max G., Happ, F. William, and Smith, Maurice P.: *Functional Teaching of the Mentally Retarded.* Springfield, Ill.: Charles C Thomas, 1967.

Physical Activities for the Mentally Retarded: Ideas for Instruction. Washington, D.C.; AAHPER, 1968.

Recreation and Physical Activity for the Mentally Retarded. Washington, D.C.: Council for Exceptional Children and AAHPER, 1966.

Van Witsen, Betty: *Perceptual Training Activities Handbook.* Columbia University, N.Y.: Teacher's College Press, 1967.

Index